Anonymous

Our Knowledge Box

Anonymous

Our Knowledge Box

ISBN/EAN: 9783337256906

Printed in Europe, USA, Canada, Australia, Japan

Cover: Foto ©ninafisch / pixelio.de

More available books at **www.hansebooks.com**

OUR KNOWLEDGE BOX:

OR,

OLD SECRETS

AND

NEW DISCOVERIES.

*A COMPENDIUM OF VALUABLE INFORMATION, AND
AN INDISPENSABLE HAND-BOOK FOR THE USE
OF EVERYBODY: THE BEST COLLECTION
OF RARE AND VALUABLE RECIPES
EVER PUBLISHED.*

———◆●◀———

GEO. BLACKIE & CO.,
Publishers,
746 BROADWAY, NEW YORK.

CONTENTS.

ᕯUR ᕯNOWLEDGE ᕯOX.

SECRETS OF THE LIQUOR TRADE.

Cider Without Apples.—To each gallon of cold water, put 1 lb. common sugar, ½ oz. tartaric acid, 1 tablespoonful of yeast, shake well, make in the evening, and it will be fit for use next day. I make in a keg a few gallons at a time, leaving a few quarts to make into next time; not using yeast again until the keg needs rinsing. If it gets a little sour make a little more into it, or put as much water with it as there is cider, and put it with the vinegar. If it is desired to bottle this cider by manufacturers of small drinks, you will proceed as follows: Put in a barrel 5 gallons hot water, 30 lbs. brown sugar, ¾ lb. tartaric acid, 25 gallons cold water, 3 pints of hop or brewers' yeast worked into paste with ¾ lb. flour, and 1 pint water will be required in making this paste, put altogether in a barrel, which it will fill, and let it work 24 hours— the yeast running out at the bung all the time, by putting in a little occasionally to keep it full. Then bottle, putting in 2 or 3 broken raisins to each bottle, and it will nearly equal Champagne.

Cider Champagne, No. 1.—Good cider, 20 gallons; spirits, 1 gallon; honey or sugar, 6 lbs. Mix, and let them rest for a fortnight; then fine with skimmed milk, 1 quart. This, put up in champagne bottles, silvered and labeled, has often been sold for Champagne. It opens very sparkling.

Cider—To Keep Sweet.—1st. By putting into the barrel before the cider has begun to work, about half a pint of whole fresh mustard seed tied up in a coarse muslin bag. 2d. By burning a little sulphur or sulphur match in the barrel previous to putting in the cider. 3d. By the use of ¾ of an ounce of the bi-sulphite of lime to the barrel. This article is the preserving powder sold at rather a high price by various firms.

To Neutralize Whiskey to make various Liquors.—To 40 gallons of whiskey, add 1½ lbs. unslacked lime; ¾ lb. alum, and ⅛ pint of spirits of nitre. Stand 24 hours and draw it off.

Madeira Wine.—To 40 gallons prepared cider, add, ¼ lb. tartaric acid; 4 gallons spirits; 3 lbs. loaf sugar. Let it stand 10 days, draw it off carefully; fine it down, and again rack it into another cask.

Sherry Wine.—To 40 gallons prepared cider, add, 2 gallons spirits; 3 lbs. of raisins; 6 gallons good sherry, and ½ ounce oil bitter almonds, (dissolved in alcohol). Let it stand 10 days, and draw it off carefully; fine it down and again rack it into another cask.

Port Wine.—To 40 gallons prepared cider, add, 6 gallons good port wine; 10 quarts wild grapes, (clusters); ½ lb. bruised rhatany root; 3 oz. tincture of kino; 3 lbs. loaf sugar; 2 gallons spirits. Let this stand ten days; color if too light, with tincture of rhatany, then rack it off and fine it. This should be repeated until the color is perfect and the liquid clear.

To correct a bad Taste and sourness in Wine.—Put in a bag the root of wild horse-radish cut in bits. Let it down in the wine, and leave it there two days; take this out, and put another, repeating the same till the wine is perfectly restored. Or fill a bag with wheat; it will have the same effect.

To restore Flat Wine.—Add four or five pounds of sugar, honey, or bruised raisins, to every hundred gallons, and bung close. A little spirits may also be added.

To restore Wine that has turned sour or sharp.—Fill a bag with leek-seed, or of leaves or twisters of vine, and put either of them to infuse in the cask.

Ginger Wine.—Take one quart of 95 per cent. alcohol, and put into it one ounce of best ginger root (bruised and not ground), five grains of capsicum, and one drachm of tartaric acid. Let stand one week and filter. Now add one gallon of water, in which one pound of crushed sugar has been boiled. Mix when cold. To make the color, boil ¼ ounce of cochineal, ¾ ounce of cream tartar, ½ ounce of saleratus, and ¼ ounce alum in a pint of water till you get a bright red color.

French Brandy.—Pure spirits, 1 gallon; best French brandy, or any kind you wish to imitate, 1 quart; loaf sugar, 2 ounces; sweet spirits of nitre, ½ ounce; a few drops of tincture of catechu, or oak bark, to roughen the taste if desired, and color to suit.

Gin.—Take 100 gallons of clean, rectified spirits; add, after you have killed the oils well, 1½ ounces of the oil of English juniper, ⅛ ounce of angelica essence, ½ ounce of the oil bitter almonds, ½ ounce of the oil of coriander, and ½ ounce of the oil of caraway; put this into the rectified spirit and well rummage it up; this is what the rectifiers call strong gin.

To make this *up*, as it is called by the trade, add 45 pounds of loaf-sugar, dissolved; then rummage the whole well up together with 4 ounces of roche alum. For finings there may be added two ounces of salts of tartar.

Aromatic Schiedam Schnapps, to imitate.—To 25 gallons good common gin, 5 over proof, add 15 pints strained honey; 2 gallons clear water; 5 pints white-sugar syrup; 5 pints spirit of nutmegs mixed with the nitric ether; 5 pints orange-flower water; 7 quarts pure water; 1 ounce acetic ether; 8 drops of oil of wintergreen, dissolved with the acetic ether. Mix all the ingredients well ; if necessary, fine with alum and salt of tartar.

St. Croix Rum.—To 40 gallons p. or n. spirits, add 2 gallons St. Croix Rum; 2 oz. acetic acid; 1½ ounce butyric acid; 3 pounds loaf sugar.

Pine-Apple Rum.—To 50 gallons rum, made by the fruit method, add 25 pine-apples sliced, and 8 pounds white sugar. Let it stand two weeks before drawing off.

Irish or Scotch Whiskey.—To 40 gallons proof spirits, add 60 drops of creosote, dissolved in 1 quart of alcohol; 2 oz. acetic acid; 1 pound loaf sugar. Stand 48 hours.

Rum Shrub.—Tartaric acid, 5 pounds; pale sugar, 100 pounds; oil lemon, 4 drs.; oil orange, 4 drs.; put them into a large cask (80 gallons), and add water, 10 gallons. Rummage till the acid and sugar are dissolved, then add rum (proof), 20 gallons; water to make up 55 gallons in all; coloring one quart or more. Fine with 12 eggs. The addition of 12 sliced oranges will improve the flavor.

Bourbon Whiskey.—To 100 gallons pure proof spirit, add 4 ounces pear oil; 2 ounces pelargonif ether; 13 drs. oil of wintergreen, dissolved in the ether; 1 gallon wine vinegar. Color with burnt sugar.

Strong Beer, English Improved.—Malt, 1 peck; coarse brown sugar, 6 pounds; hops, 4 ounces; good yeast, 1 teacup; if you have not malt, take a little over 1 peck of barley, (twice the amount of oats will do, but are not as good,) and put it into an oven after the bread is drawn, or into a stove oven, and steam the moisture from them. Grind coarsely. Now pour upon the ground malt 3½ gallons of water at 170 or 172° of heat. The tub in which you scald the malt should have a false bottom, 2 or 3 inches from the

6 *OUR KNOWLEDGE BOX.*

real bottom; the false bottom should be bored full of gimlet holes, so as to act as a strainer, to keep back the malt meal. When the water is poured on, stir them well, and let it stand 3 hours, and draw off by a faucet; put in 7 gallons more of water at 180 to 182°; stir it well, and let it stand 2 hours, and draw it off. Then put on a gallon or two of cold water, stir it well, and draw it off; you should have about 5 or 6 gallons. Put the 6 pounds of coarse brown sugar in an equal amount of water; mix with the wort, and boil 1½ to 2 hours with the hops; you should have eight gallons when boiled; when cooled to 80° put in the yeast, and let it work 18 to 20 hours, covered with a sack; use sound iron hooped kegs or porter bottles, bung or cork tight, and in two weeks it will be good sound beer, and will keep a long time; and for persons of a weak habit of body, and especially females, 1 glass of this with their meals is far better than tea or coffee, or all the ardent spirits in the universe. If more malt is used, not exceeding ½ a bushel, the beer, of course, would have more spirit, but this strength is sufficient for the use of families or invalids.

Root Beer.—For 10 gallons beer, take 3 pounds common burdock root, or 1 ounce essence of sassafras; ½ pound good hops; 1 pint corn, roasted brown. Boil the whole in 6 gallons pure water until the strength of the materials is obtained; strain while hot into a keg, adding enough cold water to make 10 gallons. When nearly cold, add clean molasses or syrup until palatable,—not sickishly sweet. Add also as much fresh yeast as will raise a batch of 8 loaves of bread. Place the keg in a cellar or other cool place, and in 48 hours you will have a keg of first-rate sparkling root beer.

Superior Ginger Beer.—Ten pounds of sugar; 9 ounces of lemon juice; ½ a pound of honey; 11 ounces of bruised ginger root; 9 gallons of water; 3 pints of yeast. Boil the ginger half an hour in a gallon of water; then add the rest of the water and the other ingredients, and strain it when cold. Add the white of an egg, beaten, and ½ an ounce of essence of lemon. Let it stand 4 days, then bottle, and it will keep many months.

Spruce Beer.—Take of the essence of spruce half a pint; bruised pimento and ginger, of each four ounces; water, three gallons. Boil five or ten minutes, then strain and add 11 gallons of warm water, a pint of yeast, and six pints of molasses. Allow the mixture to ferment for 24 hours.

To Cure Ropy Beer.—Put a handful or two of flour, and the same quantity of hops, with a little powdered alum, into the beer and rummage it well.

To give Beer the appearance of Age.—add a few handfuls of pickled cucumbers and Seville oranges, both chopped up. This is said to make malt liquor appear six months older than it really is.

How to make Mead.—The following is a good receipt for Mead :—
On twenty pounds of honey pour five gallons of boiling water; boil,
and remove the scum as it rises; add one ounce of best hops, and
boil for ten minutes; then put the liquor into a tub to cool; when
all but cold add a little yeast, spread upon a slice of toasted bread;
let it stand in a warm room. When fermentation is set up, put the
mixture into a cask, and fill up from time to time as the yeast runs
out of the bunghole; when the fermentation is finished, bung it
down, leaving a peg-hole which can afterwards be closed, and in
less than a year it will be fit to bottle.

Stomach Bitters, equal to Hostetter's, for one-fourth its cost.—Euro-
pean Gentian root, 1½ ounce; orange peel, 2½ ounces; cinnamon,
¼ ounce; aniseseed, ½ ounce; coriander seed, ½ ounce; cardamon
seed, ⅛ ounce; unground Peruvian bark, ½ ounce; gum kino, ¼
ounce; bruise all these articles, and put them into the best alcohol, 1 pint; let it stand a week and pour off the clear tincture:
then boil the dregs a few minutes in 1 quart of water, strain, and
press out all the strength; now dissolve loaf sugar, 1 pound, in the
hot liquid, adding 3 quarts cold water, and mix with spirit tincture first poured off, or you can add these, and let it stand on the
dregs if preferred.

Soda Syrup, with or without Fountains.—The common or more
watery syrups are made by using loaf or crushed sugar, 8 pounds;
pure water, 1 gallon, gum arabic, 2 ounces, mix in a brass or copper kettle; boil until the gum is dissolved, then skim and strain
through white flannel, after which add tartaric acid, 5½ oz., dissolved in hot water; to flavor, use extract of lemon, orange, rose,
pine-apple, peach, sarsaparilla, strawberry, etc., ½ ounce to each
bottle, or to your taste.

Bead for Liquor.—The best bead is the orange-flower water bead,
(oil of neroli,) 1 drop to each gallon of brandy. *Another method:*—
To every 40 drops of sulpuric acid, add 60 drops purest sweet oil
in a glass vessel; use immediately. This quantity is generally
sufficient for 10 gallons spirit. *Another:*—take 1 ounce of the
purest oil sweet almonds; 1 ounce of sulphuric acid; put them in
a stone mortar, add, by *degrees*, 2 ounces white lump sugar, rubbing it well with the pestle till it becomes a paste; then add small
quantities of spirits of wine till it comes into a liquid. This quantity is sufficient for 100 gallons. The first is strongly recommended as the best.

Coloring for Liquors.—Take 2 pounds crushed or lump sugar, put
it into a kettle that will hold 4 to 6 quarts, with ¼ tumbler of water.
Boil it until it is *black*, then take it off and cool with water, stirring it as you put in the water.

Wax Putty for Leaky Casks, Bungs, etc.—Spirits turpentine, 2 pounds; tallow, 4 pounds; solid turpentine, 12 pounds. Melt the wax and solid turpentine together over a slow fire, then add the tallow. When melted, remove far from the fire, then stir the spirits turpentine, and let it cool.

Cement for the Mouths of Corked Bottles.—Melt together ¼ of a pound of rosin, a couple of ounces of beeswax. When it froths stir it with a tallow candle. As soon as it melts, dip the mouths of the corked bottles into it. This is an excellent thing to exclude the air from such things as are injured by being exposed to it.

DRUGGISTS' DEPARTMENT.

Arnica Liniment.—Add to one pint of sweet oil, two tablespoonfuls of tincture of arnica; or the leaves may be heated in the oil over a slow fire. Good for wounds, stiff joints, rheumatic, and all injuries.

Ayer's Cherry Pectoral.—Take four grains of acetate of morphia, 2 fluid drachms of tincture of bloodroot, 7 fluid drachms each of antimonial wine and wine of ipecacuanha, and 3 fluid ounces of syrup of wild cherry. Mix.

Balm Gilead.—Balm-gilead buds, bottled up in new rum, are very healing to fresh cuts or wounds. No family should be without a bottle.

Blackberry Cordial.—To one quart of blackberry juice, add one pound of white sugar, one tablespoonful of cloves, one of allspice, one of cinnamon, and one of nutmeg. Boil all together fifteen minutes; add a wineglass of whiskey, brandy or rum. Bottle while hot, cork tight, and seal. This is almost a specific in diarrhea. One dose, which is a wineglassful for an adult—half that quantity for a child—will often cure diarrhea. It can be taken three or four times a day if the case is severe.

Brandreth's Pills.—Take two pounds of aloes, one pound of gamboge, four ounces of extract of colocynth, half a pound of castile soap, two fluid drachms of oil of peppermint, and one fluid drachm of cinnamon. Mix, and form into pills.

Brown's Bronchial Troches.—Take one pound of pulverized extract of licorice, one and a half pounds of pulverized sugar, four ounces of pulverized cubebs, four ounces of pulverized gum arabic, and one ounce of pulverized extract of conium. Mix.

Bryan's Pulmonic Wafers for Coughs, Colds, Etc.—Take white sugar, seven pounds; tincture of syrup of ipecac, four ounces: antimonial wine, two ounces; morphine, ten grains; dissolved in a tablespoonful of water, with ten or fifteen drops sulphuric acid; tincture of bloodroot, one ounce; syrup of tolu, two ounces; add these to the sugar, and mix the whole mass as confectioners do for lozenges, and cut into lozenges the ordinary size. Use from six to twelve of these in twenty-four hours. They sell at a great profit.

Candied Lemon or Peppermint, for Colds.—Boil one and a half pounds of sugar in a half pint of water, till it begins to candy round the sides; put in eight drops of essence; pour it upon buttered paper, and cut it with a knife.

Camphor Balls, for rubbing on the hands, to prevent chaps, etc. Melt three drachms of spermaceti, four drachms of white wax, and one ounce of almond oil; stir in three drachms of powdered camphor. Pour the compound into small gallipots, so as to form small hemispherical cakes. They may be colored with alkanet, if preferred.

Camphorated Oil.—This is another camphor liniment. The proportions are the same as in the preceding formula, substituting olive oil for the alcohol, and exposing the materials to a moderate heat. As an external stimulant application it is even more powerful than the spirits; and to obtain its full influence the part treated should be also covered with flannel and oil silk. It forms a valuable liniment in chronic rheumatism and other painful affections, and is specially valuable as a counter-irritant in sore or inflamed throats and diseased bowels. Camphor constitutes the basis of a large number of valuable liniments. Thus, in cases of whooping-cough and some chronic bronchitic affections, the following liniment may be advantageously rubbed into the chest and along the spine. Spirits of camphor, two parts; laudanum, half a part; spirits of turpentine, one part; castile soap in powder, finely divided, half an ounce; alcohol, 3 parts. Digest the whole together for three days, and strain through linen. This liniment should be gently warmed before using. A powerful liniment for old rheumatic pains, especially when affecting the loins, is the following: camphorated oil and spirits of turpentine, of each two parts; water of hartshorn, one part; laudanum, one part; to be well shaken together. Another very efficient liniment or embrocation, serviceable in chronic painful affections, may be conveniently and easily made as follows: Take of camphor, one ounce; cayenne pepper, in powder, two teaspoonfuls; alcohol, one pint. The whole to be digested with moderate heat for ten days, and filtered. It is an active rubificant; and after a slight friction with it, it produces a grateful, thrilling sensation of heat in the pained part, which is rapidly relieved.

Camphor Tablet for Chapped Hands, etc.—Melt tallow, and add a little powdered camphor and glycerine, with a few drops of oil of almonds to scent. Pour in molds and cool.

Camphorated Eye-Water.—Sulphate of copper, 15 grains; French bole, 15 grains; camphor, 4 grains; boiling water, 4 oz. Infuse, strain, and dilute with 2 quarts of cold water.

Canker-Cure.—Take one large teaspoonful of water, two teaspoonfuls of honey, two of loaf sugar, three of powdered sage, two of powdered gold-thread, and one of alum. Stir up all together; put into a vessel, and let it simmer moderately over a steady fire. An oven is better. Then bottle for use. Give a teaspoonful occasionally through the day.

Cephalic Snuff.—Dried asarbacca leaves, three parts; majoram, one part, lavender flowers, one part; rub together to a powder.

Certain Cure for Headache and all Neuralgic Pains.—Opodeldoc, spirits of wine, sal ammoniac, equal parts. To be applied as any other lotion.

Chamomile Pills.—Aloes, twelve grains; extract chamomile, thirty-six grains; oil of chamomile, three drops; make into twelve pills: two every night, or twice a day.

Chlorine Pastiles for Disinfecting the Breath.—Dry chloride of lime, two drachms; sugar, eight ounces; starch, one ounce, gum tragacanth, one drachm; carmine, two grains. Form into small lozenges.

2. Sugar flavored with vanilla, 1 ounce; powdered tragacanth, 20 grains; liquid chloride of soda sufficient to mix; add two drops of any essential oil. Form a paste and divide into lozenges of 15 grains each,

Cholera Morbus.—Take two ounces of the leaves of the bene plant, put them in half a pint of cold water and let them soak an hour. Give two tablespoonfuls hourly, until relief is experienced.

Cholera Remedy.—Spirits of wine, one ounce; spirits of lavender, quarter ounce; spirits of camphor, quarter ounce; compound tincture of benzoin, half an ounce; oil of origanum, quarter ounce; twenty drops on moist sugar. To be rubbed outwardly also.

2. Twenty-five *minims* of diluted sulphuric acid in an ounce of water.

Corn Remedy.—Soak a piece of copper in strong vinegar for twelve or twenty-four hours. Pour the liquid off, and bottle. Apply frequently, till the corn is removed.

2. Supercarbonate of soda, one ounce, finely pulverized, and mix with half an ounce of lard. Apply on a linen rag every night.

Cough Compound.—For the cure of coughs, colds, asthma, whooping cough and all diseases of the lungs; One spoonful of common tar, three spoonfuls of honey, the yolk of three hen's eggs, and half a pint of wine; beat the tar, eggs and honey well together with a knife, and bottle for use. A teaspoonful every morning, noon and night, before eating.

Cough Syrup.—Put one quart hoarhound to one quart water, and boil it down to a pint; add two or three sticks of licorice and a tablespoonful of essence of lemon. Take a tablespoonful of the syrup three times a day, or as often as the cough may be troublesome. The above receipt has been sold for $100. Several firms are making much money by its manufacture.

Cure for Diarrhea.—The following is said to be an excellent cure for the above distressing complaint: Laudanum, two ounces; spirits of camphor, two ounces; essence of peppermint, two ounces; Hoffman's anodyne, two ounces; tincture of cayenne pepper, two drachms; tincture of ginger, one ounce. Mix all together. Dose, teaspoonful in a little water, or a half teaspoonful repeated in an hour afterward in a tablespoonful of brandy. This preparation it is said, will check diarrhea in ten minutes, and abate other premonitory symptoms of cholera immediately. In cases of cholera, it has been used with great success to restore reaction by outward application.

Digestive Pills.—Rhubarb, two ounces; ipecacuanha, half an ounce; cayenne pepper, quarter of an ounce; soap, half an ounce; ginger, quarter of an ounce; gamboge, half an ounce. Mix, and divide into four grain pills.

Dried Herbs.—All herbs which are to be dried should be washed, separated, and carefully picked over, then spread on a coarse paper and keep in a room until perfectly dry. Those which are intended for cooking should be stripped from the stems and rubbed very fine. Then put them in bottles and cork tightly. Put those which are intended for medicinal purposes into paper bags, and keep them in a dry place.

Dysentery Specific, (particularly for bloody dysentery in Adults and Children.)—Take one pound gum arabic, one ounce gum tragacanth, dissolved in two quarts of soft water, and strained. Then take one pound of cloves, half a pound of cinnamon, half a pound allspice, and boil in two quarts of soft water, and strain. Add it to the gums, and boil all together over a moderate fire, and stir into it two pounds of loaf sugar. Strain the whole again when you take it off, and when it is cool, add to it half a pint sweet tincture rhubarb, and a pint and a half of best brandy. Cork it tight in bottles, as the gums will sour, if exposed. If corked properly it will keep for years.

Anti-Bilious Pills.—Compound extract of colocynth, 60 grains; rhubarb, 30 grains; soap, 10 grains. Make into 24 pills. Dose 2 to 4.

2. Compound extract of colocynth, 2 drachms; extract of rhubarb, half a drachm; soap, 10 grains. Mix, and divide into 40 pills. Dose, 1, 2, or 3.

3. Scammony, 10 to 15 grains; compound extract of colocynth, 2 scruples; extract of rhubarb, half a drachm; soap, 10 grains; oil of caraway, 5 drops. Make into 20 pills. Dose, 1 or 2, as required.

Great Pain Extractor.—Spirits of ammonia, one ounce; laudanum, one ounce; oil of organum, one ounce; mutton tallow, half-pound; combine the articles with the tallow when it is nearly cool.

Godfrey's Cordial.—Sassafras, six ounces; seeds of coriander, caraway and anise, of each one ounce; infuse in six pints of water; simmer the mixture till reduced to four pints; then add six pounds of molasses; boil a few minutes; when cold, add three fluid ounces of tincture of opium. For children teething.

Hydrophobia, to Prevent.—Elecampane, one drachm; chalk, four drachms; Armenian bole, three drachms; alum, ten grains; oil of aniseseed, five drops.

Infant's Syrup.—The syrup is made thus: one pound best box raisins, half an ounce of aniseseed, two sticks licorice; split the raisins, pound the aniseseed, and cut the licorice fine; add to it three quarts of rain water, and boil down to two quarts. Feed three or four times a day, as much as the child will willingly drink. The raisins are to strengthen, the anise is to expel the wind, and the licorice as a physic.

Basilicon Ointment.—Good resin, five parts; lard, eight parts; yellow wax, two parts. Melt, and stir together till cool,

Cancer Ointment.—White arsenic, sulphur, powdered flowers of lesser spearwort, and stinking chamomile, levigated together and formed into a paste with white of egg.

Elder Flower Ointment.—Lard, twenty-five pounds; prepared mutton suet, five pounds; melt in an earthen vessel; add elder flower water, three gallons. Agitate for half an hour, and set it aside; the next day gently pour off the water, remelt the ointment, add benzoic acid three drachms; otto of roses, twenty drops; essence of bergamot and oil of rosemary, of each, thirty drops; again agitate well, let it settle for a few minutes, and pour off the clear into pots.

Eruption Ointment, for Frosted Feet, etc.—Chrome yellow, and hog's lard.

Foot Ointment (for all domestic animals).—Equal parts of tar, lard and resin, melted together.

Golden Ointment.—Orpiment, mixed with lard to the consistence of an ointment.

Pile Ointment.—Powdered nutgall, two drachms; camphor, one drachm; melted wax, one ounce; tincture of opium, two drachms. Mix.

Swaim's Vermifuge.—Wormseed, two ounces: valerian, rhubarb, pink-root, white agaric, of each, one and a half ounces; boil in sufficient water to yield three quarts of decoction, and add to it thirty drops of oil of tansy, and forty-five drops of oil of cloves, dissolved in a quart of rectified spirits. Dose, one teaspoonful at night.

For Tetter, Ringworm, and Scald Head.—One pound simple cerate; sulphuric acid, one-quarter of a pound; mix together, and ready for use.

Tincture for Wounds.—Digest flowers of St. Johnswart, one handful, in half a pint of rectified spirits, then express the liquor and dissolve it in myrrh, aloes, and dragon's blood, of each one drachm, with Canada balsam, half an ounce.

Tonic.—The following is the tonic used by reformed drunkards to restore the vigor of the stomach. Take of gentian root, half an ounce; valerian root, one drachm; best rhubarb root, two drachms; bitter orange peel, three drachms; cardamom seeds, half an ounce; and cinnamon bark, one drachm. Having bruised all the above together in a mortar (the druggist will do it if requested), pour upon it one and a half pints of boiling water and cover up close; let it stand till cold; strain, bottle, and cork securely; keep in a dark place. Two tablespoonfuls may be taken every hour before meals, and half that quantity whenever the patient feels that distressing sickness and prostration so generally present for some time after alcoholic stimulants have been abandoned.

Whooping Cough.—Mix a quarter of a pound of ground elecampane root in half a pint of strained honey and half a pint of water. Put them in a glazed earthen pot, and place it in a stone oven, with half the heat required to bake bread. Let it bake until about the consistency of strained honey, and take it out. Administer in doses of a teaspoonful before each meal, to a child; if an adult, double the dose.

Wild Cherry Bitters.—Boil a pound of wild cherry bark in a quart of water till reduced to a pint. Sweeten and add a little rum to preserve, or, if to be used immediately, omit the rum. Dose, a wineglassful three times a day, on an empty stomach.

A Certain Cure for Drunkenness.—Sulphate of iron, 5 grains; magnesia, 10 grains; peppermint water, 11 drachms; spirits of nutmeg, 1 drachm; twice a day. This preparation acts as a tonic and stimulant, and so partially supplies the place of the accustomed liquor, and prevents that absolute physical and moral prostration that follows a sudden breaking off from the use of stimulating drinks.

MANUFACTURERS' DEPARTMENT.

Indelible Ink for Marking Clothing.—Nitrate of silver, five scruples; gum arabic, two drachms; sap green, one scruple; distilled water, one ounce; mix together. Before writing on the article to be marked, apply a little of the following: carbonate of soda, one-half ounce; distilled water, four ounces; let this last, which is the mordant, get dry; then, with a quill pen, write what you require.

Imitation Gold.—16 parts platina; 7 parts copper; 1 part zinc. Put in a covered crucible, with powdered charcoal, and melt together till the whole forms one mass, and are thoroughly incorporated together. Or, take 4 oz. platina, 3 oz. silver, 1 oz. copper.

Imitation Silver.—11 oz. refined nickel; 2 oz. metalic bismuth. Melt the compositions together three times, and pour them out in ley. The third time, when melting, add 2 oz. pure silver. Or take ¼ oz. copper, 1 oz. bismuth, 2 oz. saltpetre, 2 oz. common salt, 1 oz. arsenic, 1 oz. potash, 2 oz. brass, and 3 oz. pure silver. Melt all together in a crucible.

Recipe for Making Artificial Honey.—To 10 lbs. sugar add 3 lbs. water, 40 grains cream tartar, 10 drops essence peppermint, and 3 lbs. strained honey. First dissolve the sugar in water, and take off the scum; then dissolve the cream of tartar in a little warm water, which you will add with some little stirring; then add the honey; heat to a boiling point, and stir for a few minutes.

Vinegar.—Take forty gallons of soft water, six quarts of cheap molasses, and six pounds of acetic acid; put them into a barrel (an old vinegar barrel is best), and let them stand from three to ten weeks, stirring occasionally. Add a little "mother" of old vinegar if convenient. Age improves it.

Soft Soap.—Dissolve fifteen pounds of common cheap hard soap in fifteen gallons of hot water, and let it cool. Then dissolve fifteen pounds of sal soda in fifteen gallons of hot water; add six pounds of unslaked lime, and boil twenty minutes. Let it cool and settle, and then pour off the clear liquor very carefully and mix it with the soap solution. It improves it very much to add one quart of alcohol after mixing the two solutions. Smaller quantities can be made in the same proportions. If too strong, add water to suit.

Babbit's Premium Soap.—5 gals. strong ley; 5 gals water; 5 lbs. tallow; 1 lb. potash; 2 lbs. sal soda; ½ lb. rosin; 1 pt. salt; 1 pt. washing fluid. Let the water boil; then put in the articles, and boil half an hour. Stir it well while boiling, and then run into moulds. It will be ready for use as soon as cold. The above preparations are for 100 pounds of soap.

Celebrated Recipe for Silver Wash.—One ounce of nitric acid, one ten-cent piece, and one ounce of quick-silver. Put in an open glass vessel and let it stand until dissolved; then add one pint of water, and it is ready for use. Make it into a powder by adding whiting, and it may be used on brass, copper, German silver, etc.

Cement for Aquaria.—Many persons have attempted to make aquarium, but have failed on account of the extreme difficulty in making the tank resist the action of water for any length of time. Below is a recipe for a cement that can be relied upon; it is perfectly free from anything that injures the animals or plants; it sticks to glass, metal, wood, stone, etc., and hardens under water. A hundred different experiments with cements have been tried, but there is nothing like it. It is the same as that used in constructing the tanks of the Zoological Gardens, London, and is almost unknown in this country. One part, by measure, say a gill, of litharge; one gill of plaster of Paris; one gill of dry, white sand, one-third of a gill of finely-powdered resin. Sift and keep corked tight until required for use, when it is to be made into a putty by mixing in boiled oil (linseed) with a little patent dryer added. Never use it after it has been mixed (that is, with the oil) over fifteen hours. This cement can be used for marine as well as fresh water aquaria, as it resists the action of salt water. The tank can be used immediately, but it is best to give it three or four hours to dry.

Cement for Attaching Metal to Glass.—Take two ounces of a thick solution of glue, and mix it with one ounce of linseed-oil varnish, and half an ounce of pure turpentine; the whole are then boiled together in a close vessel. The two bodies should be clamped and held together for about two days after they are united, to allow the cement to become dry. The clamps may then be removed.

Cement for Mending Broken China.—Stir plaster of Paris into a thick solution of gum arabic, till it becomes a viscous paste. Apply it with a brush to the fractured edges, and draw the parts closely together.

Cement for Mending Steam Boilers.—Mix two parts of finely powdered litharge with one part of very fine sand, and one part of quicklime which has been allowed to slack spontaneously by exposure to the air. This mixture may be kept for any length of time without injury.. In using it a portion is mixed into paste with linseed oil, or, still better, boiled linseed oil. In this state it must be quickly applied, as it soon becomes hard.

Cheap White House Paint.—Take skim milk, two quarts, eight ounces fresh slaked lime, six ounces linseed oil; two ounces white Burgundy pitch, three pounds Spanish white. Slake the lime in water, expose it to the air, and mix in about one-quarter of the milk, the oil, in which the pitch is previously dissolved, to be added, a little at the time; then the rest of the milk, and afterwards the Spanish white. This quantity is sufficient for thirty square yards, two coats, and costs but a few cents. If the other colors are wanted, use, instead of Spanish white, other coloring matter.

Composition for House-Roofs.—Take one measure of fine sand, two of sifted wood-ashes, and three of lime, ground up with oil. Mix thoroughly, and lay on with a painter's brush, first a thin coat and then a thick one. This composition is not only cheap, but it strongly resists fire.

Diamond Cement.—Isinglass, one ounce; distilled vinegar, five and a half ounces; spirits of wine, two ounces; gum ammoniacum, half an ounce; gum mastic, half an ounce. Mix well.

French Polish.—To one pint of spirits of wine, add a quarter of an ounce of gum copal, quarter of an ounce of gum arabic, and one ounce of shellac. Let the gums be well bruised, and sifted through a piece of muslin. Put the spirits and the gums together in a vessel that can be closely corked; place them near a warm stove, and frequently shake them; in two or three days they will be dissolved; strain the mixture through a piece of muslin, and keep it tightly corked for use.

Furniture Oil for Polishing and Staining Mahogany.—Take of linseed oil, one gallon; alkanet root, three ounces; rose pink, one ounce. Boil them together ten minutes, and strain so that the oil be quite clear. The furniture should be well rubbed with it every day until the polish is brought up, which will be more durable than any other.

Glue for ready Use.—To any quantity of glue use common whiskey instead of water. Put both together in a bottle, cork tight, and set it away for three or four days, when it will be fit for use without the application of heat.

A Quart of Ink, for a Dime.—Buy extract of logwood, which may be had at three cents an ounce, or cheaper by the quantity. Buy also, for three cents, an ounce of *bi-chromate of potash.* Do not make a mistake, and get the simple chromate of potash. The former is orange red, and the latter clear yellow. Now, take half an ounce of extract of logwood and ten grains of bi-chromate of potash, and dissolve them in a quart of hot rain water. When cold, pour it into a glass bottle, and leave it uncorked for a week or two. Exposure to the air is indispensable. The ink is then made, and has cost five to ten minutes' labor, and about three cents, beside the bottle. The ink is at first an intense steel blue, but becomes quite black.

An Excellent Substitute for Ink.—Put a couple of iron nails into a teaspoonful of vinegar. In half an hour pour in a tablespoonful of strong tea, and then you will have ink enough for a while.

Ink, First-Rate Black.—Take twelve pounds of bruised galls, five pounds of gum Senegal, five pounds of green sulphate of iron, and twelve gallons of rain water. Boil the galls with nine gallons of water for three hours, adding fresh water to replace what is lost by evaporation. Let the decoction settle, and draw off the clear liquor; add to it a strained solution of the gum; dissolve also the sulphate of iron separately, and mix the whole.

Ink, Blue.—Chinese blue, three ounces; oxalic acid, (pure,) three-quarters of an ounce; gum arabic, powdered, one ounce; distilled water, six pints. Mix.

Ink, Cheap Printing.—Take equal parts of lampblack and oil; mix and keep on the fire till reduced to the right consistency. This is a good ink for common purposes, and is very cheap. We have used it extensively ourselves.

Ink, Copying.—Dissolve half an ounce of gum and twenty grains of Spanish licorice in thirteen drachms of water, and add one drachm of lampblack, previously mixed with a teaspoonful of sherry.

Ink, Indelible.—To four drachms of lunar caustic, in four ounces of water, add 60 drops of nutgalls, made strong by being pulverized and steeped in soft water. The mordant, which is to be applied to the cloth before writing, is composed of one ounce of pearlash, dissolved in four ounces of water, with a little gum arabic dissolved in it. Wet the spot with this; dry and iron the cloth; then write.

Ink, Indelible Marking.—One and a half drachms of nitrate of silver, one ounce of distilled water, half an ounce of strong mucilage of gum arabic, three-quarters of a drachm of liquid ammonia. Mix the above in a clean glass bottle, cork tightly, and keep in a dark place till dissolved, and ever afterwards. Directions for use: Shake the bottle, then dip a clean quill pen in the ink, and write or draw what you require on the article; immediately hold it close to the fire (without scorching), or pass a hot iron over it, and it will become a deep and indelible black, indestructible by either time or acids of any description.

Ink, Indestructible.—On many occasions it is of importance to employ an ink indestructible by any process, that will not equally destroy the material on which it is applied. For black ink, twenty-five grains of copal, in powder, are to be dissolved in two hundred grains of oil of lavender, by the assistance of a gentle heat, and are then to be mixed with two and a half grains of lampblack and half a grain of indigo. This ink is particularly useful for labelling phials, &c., containing chemical substances of a corrosive nature.

Ink for Marking Linen with Type.—Dissolve one part of asphaltum in four parts of oil of turpentine, and lamp-black or black-lead, in fine powder, in sufficient quantity to render of proper consistency to print with type.

Ink Powder for Immediate Use.—Reduce to powder ten ounces of gall-nuts, three ounces of green copperas, two ounces each of powdered alum and gum arabic. Put a little of this mixture into white wine, and it will be fit for immediate use.

Ink Stains.—The moment the ink is spilled, take a little milk, and saturate the stain, soak it up with a rag, and apply a little more milk, rubbing it well in. In a few minutes the ink will be completely removed.

Red Ink.—Take of the raspings of Brazil wood, quarter of a pound, and infuse them two or three days in colorless venegar. Boil the infusion one hour and a half over a gentle fire, and afterward filter it while hot, through paper laid in an earthenware cullender. Put it again over the fire, and dissolve in it first half an ounce of gum arabic, and afterward of alum and white sugar each half an ounce. Care should be taken that the Brazil wood be not adulterated with the Braziletto or campeachy wood.

Transfer Ink.—Mastic in tears, four ounces; shellac, six oz.; Venice turpentine, half an ounce; melt together; add wax, half a pound; tallow, three ounces. When dissolved, further add hard tallow soap (in shavings), three ounces; and when the whole is combined, add lampblack, two ounces. Mix well, cool a little, and then pour it into molds. This ink is rubbed down with a little water in a cup or saucer, in the same way as water-color cakes. In winter, the operation should be performed near the fire.

Indian Glues.—Take one pound of the best glue, the stronger the better, boil it and strain it very clear; boil also four ounces of isinglass; put the mixture into a double glue pot, add half a pound of brown sugar, and boil the whole until it gets thick; then pour it into thin plates or molds, and when cold you may cut and dry them in small pieces for the pocket. The glue is used by merely holding it over steam, or wetting it with the mouth. This is a most useful and convenient article, being much stronger than common glue. It is sold under the name of Indian glue, but is much less expensive in making, and is applicable to all kinds of small fractures, etc.; answers well on the hardest woods, and cements china, etc., though, of course, it will not resist the action of hot water. For parchment and paper, in lieu of gum or paste, it will be found equally convenient.

Japanese Cement.—Intimately mix the best powdered rice with a little cold water, then gradually add boiling water until a proper consistence is acquired, being particularly careful to keep it well stirred all the time; lastly, it must be boiled for one minute in a clean saucepan or earthern pipkin. This glue is beautifully white and almost transparent, for which reason it is well adapted for fancy paper work, which requires a strong and colorless cement.

Liquid Blacking.—Mix a quarter of a pound of ivory-black, six gills of vinegar, a tablespoonful of sweet oil, and two large spoonfuls of molasses. Stir the whole well together, and it will then be fit for use.

Liquid Glue.—Dissolve one part of powdered alum, one hundred and twenty parts of water; add one hundred and twenty parts of glue, ten of acetic acid, and forty of alcohol, and digest. Prepared glue is made by dissolving common glue in warm water, and then adding acetic acid (strong vinegar) to keep it. Dissolve one pound of best glue in one and a half pints of water, and add one pint of vinegar. It is then ready for use.

Magic Copying Paper.—To make black paper, lampblack mixed with cold lard; red paper, Venetian red mixed with lard; blue paper, Prussian blue mixed with lard; green paper, Chrome green mixed with lard. The above ingredients to be mixed to the consistency of thick paste, and to be applied to the paper with a rag. Then take a flannel rag, and rub until all color ceases coming off. Cut your sheets four inches wide and six inches long; put four sheets together, one of each color, and sell for twenty-five cents per package. The first cost will not exceed three cents.

Directions for writing with this paper: Lay down your paper

upon which you wish to write; then lay on the copying paper, and over this lay any scrap of paper you choose; then take any hard pointed substance and write as you would with a pen.

Mahogany Stain.—Break two ounces of dragon's blood in pieces, and put them in a quart of rectified spirits of wine; let the bottle stand in a warm place, and shake it frequently. When dissolved, it is fit for use, and will render common wood an excellent imitation of mahogany.

Marine Glue.—Dissolve four parts of India-rubber in thirty-four parts of coal tar naptha, aiding the solution with heat and agitation. The solution is then thick as cream, and it should be added to sixty-four parts of powdered shellac, which must be heated in the mixture till all is dissolved. While the mixture is hot it is poured on plates of metal, in sheets like leather. It can be kept in that state, and when it is required to be used, it is put into a pot and heated till it is soft, and then applied with a brush to the surfaces to be joined. Two pieces of wood joined with this cement can scarcely be sundered.

Parchment.—Paper parchment may be produced by immersing paper in a concentratic solution of chloride of zinc.

Amalgam of Gold.—Place one part of gold in a small iron saucepan or ladle, perfectly clean, then add 8 parts of mercury, and apply a gentle heat, when the gold will dissolve; agitate the mixture for one minute, and pour it out on a clean plate or stone slab.

For gilding brass, copper, etc. The metal to be gilded is first rubbed over with a solution of nitrate of mercury, and then covered with a very thin film of the amalgam. On heat being applied the mercury volatilizes, leaving the gold behind.

A much less proportion of gold is often employed than the above, where a very thin and cheap gilding is required, as by increasing the quantity of the mercury, the precious metal may be extended over a much larger surface. A similar amalgam prepared with silver is used for silvering.

Amalgam for Mirrors.—Lead and tin, each 1 oz; bismuth, 2 oz; mercury, 4 oz.; melt as before, and add the mercury. These are used to silver mirrors, glass globes, etc., by warming the glass, melting the amalgam, and applying it.

Annealing Steel.—1. For a small quantity. Heat the steel to a cherry red in a charcoal fire, then bury in sawdust, in an iron box, covering the sawdust with ashes. Let stay until cold.—2. For a larger quantity, and when it is required to be very " soft." · Pack the steel with cast iron (lathe or planer) chips in an iron box, as follows: Having at least $\frac{1}{2}$ or $\frac{3}{4}$ inch in depth of chips in the bottom of the box, put in a layer of steel, then more chips to fill spaces between the steel, and also the ½ or ¾ inch space between the sides of box and steel, then more steel; and lastly, at least 1 inch in depth of chips, well rammed down on top of steel. Heat to and keep at a red heat for from two to four hours. Do not disturb the box until cold.

To make Bell Metal.—1. Melt together under powdered charcoal, 100 parts of pure copper, with 20 parts of tin, and unite the two metals by frequently stirring the mass. Product very fine.—2. Copper 3 parts; tin 1 part; as above. Some of the finest church bells in the world have this composition.—3. Copper 2 parts: tin 1 part; as above.—4. Copper 72 parts; tin 26½ parts; iron 1½ parts. The bells of small clocks or pendules are made of this alloy in Paris.

Brass to Make. 1. *Fine Brass.*—2 parts of copper to 1 part of zinc. This is nearly one equivalent each of copper and zinc, if the equivalent of the former metal be taken at 63-2; or 2 equivalents of copper to 1 equivalent of zinc, if it be taken with Liebig and Berzelius, at 31-6.

2. Copper 4 parts, zinc 1 part. An excellent and very useful brass.

Cleansing Solution for Brass.—Put together two ounces sulphuric acid, an ounce and a half nitric acid, one dram saltpetre and two ounces rain water. Let stand for a few hours, and apply by passing the article in and out quickly, and then washing off thoroughly with clean rain water. Old, discolored brass chains treated in this way will look equally as well as when new. The usual method of drying as in sawdust.

To Cover Brass with beautiful Luster Colors.—One ounce of cream of tartar is dissolved in one quart of hot water, to which is added half an ounce of tin salt (protochloride of tin) dissolved in four ounces of cold water. The whole is then heated to boiling, the clear solution decanted from a trifling precipitate, and poured under continual stirring into a solution of three ounces hyposulphite of soda in one-half a pint of water, whereupon it is again heated to boiling, and filtered from the separated sulphur. This solution produces on brass the various luster-colors, depending on the length of time during which the articles are allowed to remain in it. The colors at first will be light to dark, gold yellow, passing through all the tints of red to an irridescent brown. A similar series of colors is produced by sulphide of copper and lead, which, however, are not remarkable for their stability; whether this defect will be obviated by the use of the tin solution, experience and time alone can show.

Bronzing Gun-Barrels.—The so-called butter of zinc used for bronzing gun-barrels is made by dissolving zinc in hydrochloric acid till no more free acid is left; which is secured by placing zinc in the acid until it ceases to be dissolved. The liquid is then evaporated until a drop taken out and placed on a piece of glass solidifies in cooling, when it is mixed with 2 parts of olive oil for every three parts of the liquid. The barrels must be cleansed and warmed before applying the so-called butter, which put on with a piece of linen rag.

Bronzing Fluid.—For brown: Iron filings, or scales, 1 lb.; arsenic, 1 oz.; hydrochloric acid, 1 lb.; metallic zinc, 1 oz. The article to be bronzed is to be dipped in this solution till the desired effect be produced.

Bronze, Green.—Acetic acid, diluted, 4 lbs; green veriter, 2 oz.; muriate of ammonia, 1 oz.; common salt, 2 oz.; alum, ½ oz.; French berries, ½ lb.; boil them together till the berries have yielded their color, and strain. Olive bronze, for brass or copper.—Nitric acid, 1 oz.; hydrochloric acid, 2 oz.; titanium or palladium, as much as will dissolve, and add three pints of distilled water.

To Soften Cast-Iron, for Drilling.—Heat to a cherry red, having it lie level in the fire, then with a pair-of cold tongs put on a piece of brimstone, a little less in size than you wish the hole to be when drilled, and it softens entirely through the piece; let it lie in the fire until a little cool, when it is ready to drill.

To Weld Cast-Iron.—Take of good clear white sand, three parts; refined solton, one part; fosterine, one part; rock-salt, one part; mix all together. Take 2 pieces of cast-iron, heat them in a moderate charcoal-fire, occasionally taking them out while heating, and dipping them into the composition, until they are of a proper heat to weld; then at once lay them on the anvil, and gently hammer them together, and, if done carefully by one who understands welding iron, you will have them nicely welded together. One man prefers heating the metal, then cooling it in the water of common beans, and heat it again for welding.

To recut old Files and Rasps.—Dissolve 4 oz. of saleratus in 1 quart of water, and boil the files in it for half an hour; then remove, wash and dry them. Now have ready, in a glass or stoneware vessel, 1 quart of rain water, into which you have slowly added 4 oz. of best sulphuric acid, and keep the proportions for any amount used. Immerse the files in this preparation for from six to twelve hours, according to fineness or coarseness of the files; then remove, wash them clean, dry quickly, and put a little sweet oil on them to cover the surface. If the files are coarse, they will need to remain in about twelve hours, but for fine files six to eight hours is sufficient. This plan is applicable to blacksmiths', gunsmiths', tinners,' coppersmiths' and machinists' files. Copper and tin workers will only require a short time to take the articles out of their files, as the soft metals with which they become filled are soon dissolved. Blacksmiths' and saw-mill files require full time. Files may be recut three times by this process. The liquid may be used at different times if required. Keep away from children, as it is poisonous.

Twist, Browning for Gun-Barrels.—Take spirits of nitre ¾ oz.; tincture of steel, ¾ oz. : (if the tincture of steel cannot be obtained, the unmedicated tincture of iron may be used, but it is not so good) black brimstone, ¼ oz.; blue vitriol, ½ oz. ; corrosive sublimate, ¼ oz.; nitric acid, 1 dr. or 60 drops; copperas, ¼ oz.; mix with 1½ pts. of rain water, keep corked, also, as the other, and the process of applying is also the same.

Gun Metal.—1. Melt together 112 lbs. of Bristol brass, 14 lbs. of spelter, and 7 lbs. of block tin.—2. Melt together 9 parts of copper and 1 part of tin; the above compounds are those used in the manufacture of small and great brass guns, swivels, etc.

Chinese Method of Mending Holes in Iron.—The Chinese mend holes in cast-iron vessels as follows : They melt a small quantity of iron in a crucible the size of a thimble, and pour the molten metal on a piece of felt covered with wood-ashes. This is pressed inside the vessel against the hole, and as it exudes on the other side it is struck by a small roll of felt covered with ashes. The new iron then adheres to the old.

Common Pewter.—Melt in a crucible 7 lbs. of tin, and when fused throw in 1 lb. of lead, 6 oz. of copper and 2 oz. of zinc. This combination of metal will form an alloy of great durability and tenacity ; also of considerable luster.

Best Pewter.—The best sort of pewter consists of 100 parts of tin, and 17 of regulus of antimony.

Hard Pewter.—Melt together 12 lbs. of tin, 1 lb. of regulus of antimony, and 4 oz. of copper.

To Mend Broken Saws.—Pure silver, 19 parts : pure copper, 1 part : pure brass, 2 parts ; all are to be filed into powder and intimately mixed. Place the saw level upon the anvil, the broken edges in close contact, and hold them so : now put a small line of the mixture along the seam, covering it with a large bulk of powdered charcoal ; now with a spirit lamp and a jeweler's blow-pipe, hold the coal-dust in place, and blow sufficient to melt the solder mixture : then with a hammer set the joint smooth, if not already so, and file away any superfluous solder ; and you will be surprised at its strength. *

Solder, to Adhere to Brass or Copper.—Prepare a soldering solution in this way: Pour a small quantity of muriatic acid on some zinc filings, so as to completely cover the zinc. Let it stand about an hour, and then pour off the acid, to which add twice its amount of water. By first wetting the brass or copper with this preparation, the solder will readily adhere.

Common Solder.—Put into a crucible 2 lbs. of lead, and when melted throw in 1 lb. of tin. This alloy is that generally known by the name of solder. When heated by a hot iron and applied to tinned iron with powdered rosin, it acts as a cement or solder.

Tempering Steel.—For tempering many kinds of tools, the steel is first hardened by heating it to a cherry red, and plunging it into cold water. Afterward the temper is drawn by moderately heating the steel again. Different degrees of hardness are required for different purposes, and the degree of heat for each of these, with the corresponding color, will be found in the annexed table:

Very pale straw color, 430°—the temper required for lancets.

A shade of darker yellow, 450°—for razors and surgical instruments.

Darker straw-yellow, 470°—for penknives.

Still darker yellow, 490°—chisels for cutting iron.

A brown yellow, 500°—axes and plane-irons.

Yellow, slightly tinged with purple, 520°—table-knives and watch-springs.

Tempering Liquid.—1. To 6 quarts of soft water put in corrosive sublimate, 1 oz.; common salt, 2 handfuls; when dissolved it is ready for use. The first gives toughness to the steel, while the latter gives the hardness. Be careful with this preparation, as it is a dangerous poison.—2. Salt, ½ teacup; saltpetre, ½ oz.; alum, pulverized, 1 tea-spoon; soft water, 1 gallon; never heat over a cherry red, nor draw any temper.—3. Saltpetre, sal-ammoniac, and alum, of each 2 oz.; salt, 1½ lbs.; water, 3 gallons, and draw no temper.—4. Saltpetre and alum, each 2 oz.; sal-ammoniac, ½ oz.; salt, 1½ lbs.; soft water, 2 gallons. Heat to a cherry red, and plunge in, drawing no temper.

Bayberry, or Myrtle Soap.—Dissolve two and a quarter pounds of white potash in five quarts of water, then mix it with ten pounds of myrtle wax, or bayberry tallow. Boil the whole over a slow fire till it turns to soap, then add a teacup of cold water; let it boil ten minutes longer; at the end of that time turn it into tin molds or pans, and let them remain a week or ten days to dry; then turn them out of the molds. If you wish to have the soap scented, stir into it an essential oil that has an agreeable smell, just before you turn it into the molds. This kind of soap is excellent for shaving, and for chapped hands : it is also good for eruptions on the face. It will be fit for use in the course of three or four weeks after it is made, but it is better for being kept ten or twelve months.

Chemical Soap, (for taking Oil, Grease, etc., from Cloth).—Take five pounds castile soap, cut fine; one pint alcohol; one pint soft water; two ounces aquafortis; one and a half ounces lampblack; two ounces of saltpetre; three ounces potash; one ounce of camphor; and four ounces of cinnamon, in powder. First dissolve the soap, potash and saltpetre, by boiling; then add all the other articles, and continue to stir until it cools; then pour into a box and let it stand twenty-four hours and cut into cakes.

Cold Soap.—Mix twenty-six pounds of melted and strained grease with four pailfuls of ley, made of twenty pounds of white potash. Let the whole stand in the sun, stirring it frequently. In the course of the week, fill the barrel with weak ley.

Genuine Erasive Soap.—Two pounds of good castile soap; half a pound of carbonate of potash ; dissolve in half a pint of hot water. Cut the soap in thin slices, and boil the soap with the potash until it is thick enough to mould in cakes; also add alcohol, half an ounce; camphor, half an ounce; hartshorn, half an ounce; color with half an ounce of pulverized charcoal.

Hard White Soap.—To fifteen pounds of lard or suet, made boiling hot, add slowly six gallons of hot ley, or solution of potash, that will bear up an egg high enough to leave a piece big as a shilling bare. Take out a little, and cool it. If no grease rise it is done. If any grease appears, add ley, and boil till no grease rises. Add three quarts of fine salt, and boil up again. If this does not harden well on cooling, add more salt. If it is to be perfumed, melt it next day, add the perfume, and run it in molds or cut in cakes.

Labor-Saving Soap.—Take two pounds of sal-soda, two pounds of yellow bar soap, and ten quarts of water. Cut the soap in thin slices, and boil together for two hours; strain, and it will be fit for use. Put the clothes in soak the night before you wash, and to every pail of water in which you boil them, add a pound of soap. They will need no rubbing; merely rinse them out, and they will be perfectly clean and white.

To Make Good Soap.—To make matchless soap, take one gallon of soft soap, to which add a gill of common salt, and boil an hour. When cold, separate the ley from the crude. Add to the crude two pounds of sal-soda, and boil in two gallons of soft water till dissolved. If you wish it better, slice two pounds of common bar soap and dissolve in the above. If the soft soap makes more than three pounds of crude, add in proportion to the sal-soda and water.

To Make Hard Soap from Soft.—Take seven pounds of good soft soap; four pounds sal-soda; two ounces borax; one ounce hartshorn; half a pound of resin; to be dissolved in twenty-two quarts of water, and boiled about twenty minutes.

Whale Oil Soap (for the destruction of Insects.)—Render common ley caustic, by boiling it at full strength on quicklime; then take the ley and boil it with as much whale oil foot as it will saponify (change to soap), pour off into molds, and, when cold, it is tolerably hard. Whale oil foot is the sediment produced in refining whale oil, and is worth two dollars per barrel.

Soluble Glass.—Mix ten parts of carbonate of potash, fifteen parts of powdered quartz, and one pound of charcoal. Fuse well together. The mass is soluble in four or five parts of boiling water, and the filtered solution, evaporated to dryness, yields a transparent glass, permanent in the air.

To Make Eggs of Pharaoh's Serpents.—Take mercury and dissolve it in moderately diluted nitric acid by means of heat, taking care, however, that there be always an excess of metallic mercury remaining; decant the solution and pour it into a solution of sulphocyanide of ammonium or potassium, which may be bought at a good drug store, or of a dealer in chemicals. Equal weights of both will answer. A precipitate will fall to the bottom of the beaker or jar, which is to be collected on a filter and washed two or three times with water, when it is put in a warm place to dry. Take for every pound of this material one ounce of gum tragacanth which has been soaked in hot water. When the gum is completely softened it is to be transferred to a mortar, and the pulverized and dried precipitate gradually mixed with it by means of a little water, so as to present a somewhat dry pill mass, from which by hand pellets of the desired size are formed, put on a piece of glass, and dried again; they are then ready for use.

Tracing Paper.—In order to prepare a beautiful transparent, colorless paper, it is best to employ the varnish formed with Demarara resin in the following way: The sheets intended for this purpose are laid flat on each other, and the varnish spread over the uppermost sheet with a brush, until the paper appears perfectly colorless, without, however, the liquid thereon being visible. The first sheet is then removed, hung up for drying, and the second treated in the same manner. After being dried, this paper is capable of being written on, either with chalk or pencil, or steel pens. It preserves its colorless transparency without becoming yellow, as is frequontly tho caso with that prepared in any other way.

Unsurpassable Blacking.—Put ono gallon of vinegar into a stone jug, and ono pound of ivory-black well pulverized, half a pound of loaf sugar, half an ounce of oil of vitriol, and seven ounces of swoot oil. Incorporato tho wholo by stirring.

2. Take twelvo ounces each of ivory-black and molasses; spermaceti oil, four ounces; and white wino vinegar, two quarts. Mix thoroughly. This contains no vitriol, and thereforo will not injuro tho leather. The trouble of making it is very little, and it would bo well to prepare it for ono's self, wero it only to bo assured that it is not injurious.

Varnish for Iron Work.—To make a good black varnish for iron work, tako eight pounds of asphaltum and fuse it in an iron kettle; then add five gallons of boilod linseed oil, ono pound of litharge, half a pound of sulphato of zinc (add theso slowly, or it will fumo over), and boil thom for about threo hours. Now add one and a half pounds of dark gum amber, and boil for two hours longer, or until tho mass will becomo quito thick when cool, after which it should bo thinned with turpentine to due consistency.

• ___

THE TOILET, PERFUMERY, Etc.

Hair Restorers and Invigorators.—There aro hundreds; Lyon's, Wood's, Barry's, Bogle's, Jayne's, Storr's, Baker's, Driscol's, Phalon's, Haskel's, Allen's, Spaulding's, etc. But, though all under different names, are similar in principle, boing vegetable oils dissolved in alcohol, with tho addition of spirit of soap, and an astringent material, such as tincturo of catechu, or infusion of bark. Tho best is to dissolvo ono ounce of castor oil in ono quart of 95 alcohol, and add ono ounce of tincturo of cantharides, two ounces of tincture of catechu, two ounces of lemon juico, two ounces of tincturo of cinchona; and to scent it, add oil of cinnamon, or oil of rosemary, or both.

To Make the Hair Soft and Glossy.—Put ono ounce of castor oil in ono pint of bay rum or alcohol, and color it with a little of tho tincturo of alkanet root. Apply a little cvery morning.

Instantaneous Hair Dye.—Tako ono drachm of nitrato of silver, and add to it just sufficient rain water to dissolvo it, *and no more;* then tako strong spirit of ammonia, and gradually pour on tho solution of silver, until it becomes as clear as water, *(the addition of the ammonia at first makes it brown)* ; then wrap round the bottle two or three covers of blue paper, to exclude the light—otherwise it will spoil. Having made this, obtain two drachms of gallic acid; put this into another bottle which will contain one-half pint; pour upon it hot water, and let it stand until cold—when it is fit for use.

Directions to Dye the Hair.—First wash the head, beard, or moustaches with soap and water; afterwards with clean water. Dry, and apply the gallic acid solution, with a clean brush. When it is almost dry, take a small tooth comb, and with a fine brush, put on the teeth of the comb a little of the silver solution, and comb it through the hair, when it will become a brilliant jet black. Wait a few hours; then wash the head again with clean water. If you want to make a brown dye, add double or treble the quantity of water to the silver solution, and you can obtain any shade of color you choose.

To Prevent Gray Hair.—When the hair begins to change color, the use of the following pomade has a beneficial effect in preventing the disease extending, and has the character of even restoring the color of the hair in many instances: Lard, 4 ounces: spermaceti, 4 drachms: oxide of bismuth, 4 drachms. Melt the lard and spermaceti together, and when getting cold stir in the bismuth; to this can be added any kind of perfume, according to choice. It should be used whenever the hair requires dressing. It must not be imagined that any good effect speedily results; it is, in general, a long time taking place, the change being very gradual.

Liquid Rouge for the Complexion.—Four ounces of alcohol, two ounces of water, twenty grains of carmine; twenty grains of ammonia, six grains of oxalic acid, six grains of alum—mix.

Vinegar Rouge.—Cochineal, three drachms; carmine lake, three drachms; alcohol, six drachms; mix, and then put into one pint of vinegar, perfumed with lavender; let it stand a fortnight, then strain for use.

Pearl Powder for Complexion.—Take white bismuth, one pound; starch powder, one ounce; orris powder, one ounce. Mix and sift through lawn. Add a drop of otto of roses or neroli.

Pearl Water for the Complexion.—Castile soap, one pound; water, one gallon. Dissolve, then add alcohol, one quart; oil of rosemary and oil of lavender, each two drachms. Mix well.

Complexion Pomatum.—Mutton grease, one pound; oxide of bismuth, four ounces; ·powdered French chalk, two ounces; mix.

Feuchtwanger's Tooth Paste.—Powdered myrrh, two ounces; burnt alum, one ounce; cream tartar, one ounce; cuttlefish bone, four ounces: drop lake, two ounces; honey, half a gallon; mix.

Spanish Vermilion for the Toilette.—Take an alkine solution of bastard saffron, and precipitate the color with lemon juice; mix the precipitate with a sufficient quantity of finely powdered French chalk and lemon juice, then add a little perfume.

Fine Tooth Powder.—Powdered orris root, one ounce; peruvian bark, one ounce; prepared chalk, one ounce; myrrh, one-half ounce.

To Make Brown Teeth White.—Apply carefully over the teeth, a stick dipped in strong acetic or nitric acid, and immediately wash out the mouth with cold water. To make the teeth even, if irregular, draw a piece of fine cord betwixt them.

Superior Cologne Water.—Alcohol, one gallon: add oil of cloves, lemon, nutmeg and bergamot, each one drachm; oil neroli, three and a half drachms; seven drops of oils of rosemary, lavender and cassia; half a pint of spirits of nitre; half a pint of elder-flower water. Let it stand a day or two, then take a cullender and at the bottom lay a piece of white cloth, and fill it up, one-fourth of white sand, and filter through it.

Smelling Salts.—Super carbonate of ammonia, eight parts; put it in coarse powder into a bottle, and pour out lavender oil one part.

Oil of Roses—for the Hair.—Olive oil, two pints: otto of roses, one drachm; oil of rosemary, one drachm; mix. It may be colored by steeping a little alkanet root in the oil (by heat) before scenting it.

Arnica Hair Wash.—When the hair is falling off and becoming thin, from the too frequent use of castor, Macassar oils, &c., or when premature baldness arises from illness, the arnica hair wash will be found of great service in arresting the mischief. It is thus prepared: take elder water, half a pint; sherry wine, half a pint; tincture of arnica, half an ounce; alcoholic ammonia, 1 drachm—if this last named ingredient is old, and has lost its strength, then two drachms instead of one may be employed. The whole of these are to be mixed in a lotion bottle, and applied every night to the head with a sponge. Wash the head with warm water twice a week. Soft brushes only must be used during the growth of the young hair.

Ammoniacal Pomatum for Promoting the Growth of Hair.—Take almond oil, quarter of a pound; white wax, half an ounce; clarified lard, three ounces; liquid ammonia, a quarter fluid ounce; otto of lavender, and cloves, of each one drachm. Place the oil, wax and lard in a jar, which set in boiling water; when the wax is melted, allow the grease to cool till nearly ready to set, then stir in the ammonia and the perfume, and put into small jars for use. Never use a hard brush, nor comb the hair too much. Apply the pomade at night only.

Bandoline for the Hair.—This mixture is best made a little at a time. Pour a tablespoonful of boiling water on a dozen quince seeds, and repeat when fresh is required.

Artificial Bear's Grease.—Bear's grease is imitated by a mixture of prepared veal suet and beef marrow. It may be scented at pleasure. The following are some of the best compounds sold by that name:

1. Prepared suets, 3 ounces; lard, 1 ounce; olive oil, 1 ounce; oil of cloves, 10 drops; compound tincture of benzoin, 1 drachm. Mix.

2. Lard, 1 pound; solution of carbonate of potash, 2 ounces. Mix.

3. Olive oil, 3 pints; white wax, 3 ounces; spermaceti, 1 ounce; scent with oil of roses and oil of bitter almonds.

Bears' Oil.—The best description of lard oil, properly perfumed, is far preferable to any other kind of oil.

Cosmetic Soap, for Washing the Hands.—Take a pound of castile soap, or any other nice old soap; scrape it fine; put it on the fire with a little water, stir it to a smooth paste; turn it into a bowl; or any kind of essence; beat it with a silver spoon till well mixed; thicken it with Indian meal, and keep it in small pots, closely covered; exposure to the air will harden it.

Cosmetic Wash for the Hair.—Red wine, one pound; salt, one drachm; sulphate of iron, two drachms; boil for a few minutes, add common verdigris, one drachm; leave it on the fire two minutes; withdraw it, and add two drachms of powdered nutgall. Rub the hair with the liquid, in a few minutes dry it with a warm cloth, and afterwards wash with water.

To Remove Dandruff.—Take a thimbleful of powdered refined borax, let it dissolve in a teacupful of water, first brush the head well, then wet a brush and apply it to the head. Do this every day for a week, and twice a week for a few times, and you will effectually remove the dandruff.

To Make the Complexion Fair.—Take emulsion of bitter almonds, one pint; oxymuriate of quicksilver, two and a half grains; sal ammonia, one drachm. Use moderately for pimples, freckles, tanned complexions.

Eau de Cologne—Cologne Water.—Oil of lavender, oil of bergamot, oil of lemon, oil of neroli, each one ounce; oil of cinnamon, half an ounce; spirit of rosemary, fifteen ounces; highly rectified spirits, eight pints. 'Let them stand fourteen days; then distil in a water bath.

2. Essential oils of bergamot, lemon, neroli, orange-peel and rosemary, each twelve drops; cardamon seeds, one drachm, rectified spirits, one pint. It improves by age,

Eau de Rosieres.—Spirits of roses, 4 pints; spirits of jessamine, one pint; spirits of orange flowers, one pint; spirits of cucumber, two and a quarter pints; spirits of celery seed, two and a quarter pints; spirits of angelica root, two and three quarter pints; tincture of benzoin, three quarters of a pint; balsam of Mecca, a few drops.

Eau de Violettes.—Macerate five ounces of fine orris root in a quart of rectified spirits, for some days, and filter.

Esprit de Bouquet.—Oil of lavender, oil of cloves and oil of bergamot, each two drachms; otto of rose, and oil of cinnamon, each, twenty drops; essence of musk, one drachm; rectified spirits, one pint. Mix.

Essence of Ambergris.—Spirits of wine, half a pint; ambergris, 24 grains. Let it stand for three days in a warm place, and filter.

Essence of Bergamot.—Spirits of wine, half a pint; bergamot-peel, four ounces: as above.

Essence of Cedrat.—Essence of bergamot, one ounce; essence of neroli, two drachms.

Essence of Cloves.—Spirits of wine, half a pint; bruised cloves, one ounce.

Essence for the Headache.—Spirits of wine, two pounds; roche alum, in fine powder, two ounces; camphor, four ounces; essence of lemon, half an ounce; strong water of ammonia, four ounces. Stop the bottle close, and shake it daily, for three or four days.

Essence of Lavender.—Essential oil of lavender, three and a half ounces; rectified spirits, two quarts; rose water, half a pint; tincture of orris, half a pint.

Essence of Lemon.—Spirits of wine, half a pint; fresh lemon-peel, four ounces.

Essence of Musk.—Take one pint proof spirit, and add two drachms musk. Let it stand a fortnight, with frequent agitation.

Essence of Neroli.—Spirits of wine, half a pint; orange-peel, cut small, three ounces; orris root in powder, one drachm; musk, two grains.

Essence for Smelling Bottles.—Oil of lavender and essence of bergamot, each one drachm; oil of orange-peel, eight drops; oil of cinnamon, four drops; oil of neroli, two drops; alcohol and strongest water of ammonia, each two ounces.

Essence of Verbena Leaf.—Take rectified spirits of wine, half a pint; otto of verbena, half a drachm; otto of bergamot, one drachm; tincture of tolu, quarter of an ounce. Mix them together, and it is ready for use. This sweet scent does not stain the handkerchief and is very economical. ·

Essence of Violets.—Spirits of wine, half a pint; orris root, one ounce. Other essences in the same manner.

Eye Water.—Take one pint of rose water, and add one teaspoonful each of spirits of camphor and laudanum. Mix and bottle. To be shaken and applied to the eyes as often as necessary. Perfectly harmless. •

Honey Water.—Rectified spirits, eight pints; oil of cloves, oil of lavender, oil of bergamot, each half an ounce; musk, eight grains; yellow sandus shavings, four ounces; digest for eight days and add two pints each of orange flower and rose water.

Lavender Water.—Oil of lavender, four ounces; spirit, three quarts; rose water, one pint, Mix and filter.

Lisbon Water.—To rectified spirit, one gallon, add essential oils of orange-peel and lemon-peel, of each three ounces, and otto of roses, one quarter of an ounce.

Odoriferous Lavender Water.—Rectified spirit, five gallons; essential oil of lavender, twenty ounces; oil of bergamot, five ounces; essence of ambergris, half an ounce.

2. Oil of lavender, three drachms; oil of bergamot, twenty drops; nerolic, six drops; otto of roses, six drops; essence of cedrat, eight drops; essence of musk, twenty drops; rectified spirit, twenty-eight fluid ounces; distilled water, four ounces.

Queen of Hungary's Water.—Spirit of rosemary, four pints; orange flower water, one quarter of a pint; essence of neroli, four drops.

FACE PAINTS.

Almond Bloom.—Boil one ounce of Brazil dust in three pints of distilled water, and strain ; add six drachms of isinglass, 2 drachms of cochineal, one ounce of alum, and eight drachms of borax ; boil again and strain through a fine cloth.

Fine Carmine—(prepared from cochineal) is used alone, or deduced with starch, &c. And also the coloring matter of safflower and other vegetable colors, in the form of pink saucers, &c.

Face Powder.—Starch, one pound ; oxide of bismuth, four ounces.

Face Whites.—French chalk is one of the most innocent ; finely powdered. White starch is also used.

Rouge.—Mix vermillion with enough gum tragacanth dissolved in water to form a thin paste ; add a few drops of almond oil, place the mixture in rouge pots, and dry by a very gentle heat.

Turkish Rouge.—Take half pint alcohol and one ounce of alkanet ; macerate ten days and pour off the liquid, which should be bottled. This is the simplest and one of the best articles of the kind.

Caution.—White lead, and all cosmetic powders containing it should never be applied to the skin, as it is the most dangerous article that could be used.

Mouth Pastiles, for Perfuming the Breath.—Extract of licorice, three ounces ; oil of cloves, one and a half drachms ; oil of cinnamon, fifteen drops. Mix, and divide into one-grain pills, and silver them.

2. Catechu, seven drachms ; orris powder, forty grains ; sugar, three ounces ; oil of rosemary, (or of clove, peppermint, or cinnamon,) four drops. Mix, and roll flat on an oiled marble slab, and cut into very small lozenges.

Oil for the Hair.—A very excellent ready-made oil for the hair which answers all common purposes, is made by mixing one part brandy with three parts of sweet oil. Add any scent you prefer.

Oil of Roses.—Fine olive oil, one pint ; otto of roses, sixteen drops. If required red, color with alkanet root, and strain before adding the otto. For common sale essence of bergamot or of lemon is often substituted, wholly or in part, for the expensive otto.

2

HUNTERS' AND TRAPPERS' SECRETS.

The following secret applies to *all* animals, as every animal is attracted by the peculiar odor in a greater or less degree; but it is best adapted to land animals, such as Foxes, Minks, Sables, Martins, Wolves, Bears, Wild Cats, &c., &c.

Take one half pound strained honey, one quarter drachm musk, three drachms oil of lavender, and four pounds of tallow, mix the whole thoroughly together, and make it into forty pills, or balls, and place one of these pills under the pan of each trap when setting it.

The above preparation will most wonderfully attract all kinds of animals, and trappers and others who use it will be sure of success.

To Catch Foxes.—Take oil of amber, and beaver's oil, each equal parts, and rub them over the trap before setting it. Set in the usual way.

To Catch Mink.—Take oil of amber, and beaver's oil, and rub over the trap. Bait with fish or birds.

To Catch Muskrat.—In the female muskrat near the vagina is a small bag which holds from 30 to 40 drops. Now all the trapper has to do, is to procure a few female muskrats and squeeze the contents of a bag into a vial. Now, when in quest of muskrats, sprinkle a few drops of the liquid on the bushes over and around the trap. This will attract the male muskrats in large numbers, and if the traps are properly arranged, large numbers of them may be taken.

⁎⁎ In trapping Muskrats, steel traps should be used, and they should be set in the paths and runs of the animal, where they come upon the banks, and in every case the trap should be set under the water, and carefully concealed; and care should be taken that it has sufficient length of chain to enable the animals to reach the water after being caught, otherwise they are liable to escape by tearing or gnawing off their legs.

To Catch Beaver.—In trapping for beaver, set the trap at the edge of the water or dam, at the point where the animals pass from deep to shoal water, and always beneath the surface, and fasten it by means of a stout chain to a picket driven in the bank, or to a bush or tree. A flat stick should be made fast to the trap by a cord a few feet long, which, if the animal chanced to carry away the trap, would float on the water and point out its position. The trap should then be baited with the following preparation, called

" *The Beaver Medicine.*"

This is prepared from a substance called castor, and is obtained from the glandulous pouches of the *male* animal.

The contents of five or six of these castor bags are mixed with a nutmeg, twelve or fifteen cloves and thirty grains of cinnamon in fine powder, and the whole well stirred together with as much whiskey as will give it the consistency of mixed mustard. This preparation must be left closely corked up, and in four or five days the odor becomes powerful; and this medicine smeared upon the bits of wood, &c., with which the traps are baited, will attract the beaver from a great distance, and wishing to make a close inspection, the animal puts its legs into the trap and is caught.

** The same caution in regard to length of chain should be observed for Beaver, as for Otters, Muskrats, &c., for unless they can reach the water they are liable to get out of the trap and escape.

Chinese Art of Catching Fish.—Take Cocculus Indicus, pulverize and mix with dough, then scatter it broadcast over the water, as you would sow seed. The fish will seize it with great avidity, and will instantly become so intoxicated that they will turn belly up on top of the water, by dozens, hundreds, or thousands, as the case may be. All that you now have to do, is to have a boat, or other convenience to gather them up, and as you gather put them in a tub of clean water and presently they will be as lively and healthy as ever.

This means of taking fish, and the manner of doing it, has, heretofore, been known to but few. The value of such knowledge admits of no question. This manner of taking fish does not injure the flesh in the least.

Secret Art of Catching fish.—Put the oil of rhodium on the bait, when fishing with the hook, and you will always succeed.

To Catch Fish.—Take the juice of smallage or lovage, and mix with any kind of bait. As long as there remain any kind of fish within many yards of your hook, you will find yourself busy pulling them out.

To Catch Abundance of Eels, Fish, &c.—Get over the water after dark, with a light and a dead fish that has been smeared with the juice of stinking glawdin—the fish will gather round you in large quantities, and can easily be scooped up.

THE FINE ARTS AND SCIENCES.

To Transfer Engravings to Plaster Casts.—Cover the plate with ink, polish its surface in the usual way, then put a wall of paper round; then pour on it some fine paste made with plaster of Paris. Jerk it to drive out the air bubbles, and let it stand one hour, when you have a fine impression.

The New and Beautiful Art of Transferring on to Glass.—Colored or plain Engravings, Photographs, Lithographs, Water Colors, Oil Colors, Crayons, Steel Plates, Newspaper Cuts, Mezzotinto, Pencil, Writing, Show Cards, Labels,—or in fact anything.

Directions.—Take glass that is perfectly clear—window glass will answer—clean it thoroughly; then varnish it, taking care to have it perfectly smooth; place it where it will be entirely free from dust; let it stand over night; then take your engraving, lay it in clear water until it is wet through (say ten or fifteen minutes), then lay it upon a newspaper, that the moisture may *dry from the surface*, and still keep the other side damp. Immediately varnish your glass the *second* time, then place your engraving on it, pressing it down firmly, so as to exclude every particle of air; next rub the paper from the back, until it is of uniform thickness—so thin that you can see through it, then varnish it the *third* time, and let it dry.

Materials Used for the Above Art.—Take two ounces balsam of fir, to one ounce of spirits of turpentine; apply with a camel's hair brush.

To Make Wax Flowers.—The following articles will be required to commence wax work: 2 lbs. white wax, ¼ lb. hair wire, 1 bottle carmine, 1 ultramarine blue, 1 bottle chrome yellow, 2 bottles chrome green, No. 1; 2 bottles chrome green, No. 2; 1 bottle rose pink, 1 bottle royal purple, 1 bottle scarlet powder, 1 bottle balsam fir, 2 dozen sheets white wax. This will do to begin with. Now have a clean tin dish and pour therein a quart or two of water; then put in about 1 lb. of the white wax and let it boil; when cool enough, so the bubbles will not form on top, it is ready to sheet, which is done as follows:—Take half of a window pane, 7x9, and, after having washed it clean, dip into a dish containing weak soapsuds; then dip into the wax and draw out steadily and plunge it into the suds, when the sheet will readily come off. Lay it on a cloth or clean paper to dry. Proceed in like manner until you have enough of the white; then add enough of the green powder to make a bright color, and heat and stir thoroughly until the color is evenly distributed; then proceed as for sheeting white wax. The other colors are rubbed into the leaves after they are cut out, rubbing light or heavy according to shade.

For patterns you can use any natural leaf, forming the creases in wax with the thumb nail or a needle; to put the flowers together or the leaves on to the stem, hold in the hand until warm enough to stick. If the sheeted wax is to be used in Summer, put in a little balsam of fir to make it hard. If for Winter, none will be required.

You can make many flowers without a teacher; but one to assist, in the commencement, would be a great help; though the most particular thing about it is to get the wax sheeted. The materials I have suggested can be procured at any drug store, and will cost from $3 to $4.50.

How to Charm Those Whom You Meet and Love.—When you desire to make any one "Love" you with whom you meet, although not personally acquainted with him, you can very readily reach him and make his acquaintance, if you observe the foregoing instructions, in addition to the following directions : Suppose you see him coming towards you in an unoccupied mood, or is recklessly, or passively walking past you, all that remains for you to do at that moment is to concentrate your thought and send it into him as before explained ; and, to your astonishment, if he was passive, he will look at you, and now is your time to send a thrill to his heart, by looking him carelessly, though determinately, into his eyes, and praying with all your heart, mind, soul and strength, that he may read your thought, and receive your true Love, which God designs we should bear one another. This accomplished, and you need not and must not wait for a cold-hearted, fashionable, and popular Christian introduction ; neither should you hastily run into his arms, but continue operating in this psychological manner ; not losing any convenient opportunity to meet him at an appropriate place, when an unembarrassed exchange of words will open the door, to the one so magnetized. At this interview, unless prudence sanction it, do not shake hands, but let your manners and loving eyes speak with Christian charity and ease ; wherever, or whenever you meet again, at the first opportunity grasp his hand, in an earnest, sincere and affectionate manner, observing at the same time, the following important directions, viz. :—As you take his bare hand in yours, press your thumb gently, though firmly, between the bones of the thumb and forefinger of his hand, and at the very instant when you press thus on the blood vessels, (which you can before ascertain to pulsate,) look him earnestly and lovingly, though not pertly or fiercely, into his eyes, and send all your heart's, mind's and soul's strength into his organization, and he will be your friend, and if you find him not to be congenial, you have him in your power, and by carefully guarding against evil influences, you can reform him to suit your own purified, Christian, and loving taste.

Mesmerism.—If you desire to mesmerise a person, who has never been put into that state, nor in the least affected, the plan is to set him in an easy posture, and request him to be calm and resigned. Take him by both hands, or else by one hand and place your other gently on his forehead. But with whatever part of his body you choose to come in contact, be sure to always touch two points, answering to the *positive* and *negative* forces. Having taken him by both hands, fix your eyes upon his, and, if possible, let him contentedly and steadily look you in the face. Remain in this position until his eyes close. Then place both your hands on his head, gently pass them to his shoulders, down the arms, and off at the ends of his fingers. Throw your hands outward as you return them to his head, and continue these passes till he can hear no voice but yours. He is then entirely in the mesmeric state. When a person is in the mesmeric state, whether put there by yourself or some one else, you can awake him by the upward passes: or else do it by an impression, as follows: Tell him, "I will count *three*, and at the same instant I say *three*, I will slap my hands together, and you will be wide awake and in your perfect senses. Are you ready?" If he answers in the affirmative, you will proceed to count " *one*, TWO, THREE!" The word *three* should be spoken suddenly, and in a very loud voice, and at the same instant the palms of the hands should be smitten together. This will instantly awake him.

To Make Magic Photographs.—Take, in the first place, an ordinary print—a card-picture, for instance—on albumen paper, beneath the negative in the usual way, and, when sufficiently printed, let it be carefully washed in the dark room, so as to remove all the free nitrate of silver, etc. Now immerse it in the following solution, also in the dark room: saturated solution bichloride of mercury (corrosive sublimate), one ounce; hydrochloric acid, one drachm. The saturated solution is previously prepared by putting into water more bichloride of mercury than it will dissolve by shaking in about twelve hours. The print will gradually be bleached in this liquid, in the ordinary meaning of the word—that is, it will disappear; but the fact is, the print is still there—its color alone is changed, a double salt having been formed of mercury and silver, which is white, as many of our readers, who have been in the habit of intensifying with a mercurial salt, are aware. As soon as the print has quite disappeared, the paper is thoroughly washed and dried in the dark room; it is also preserved between folds of orange-colored paper, in order to keep it from the action of light, for the surface is still in some measure sensitive to light. The bleaching of the print—that is, its conversion into a white salt—is effected more quickly by keeping it in motion in the mercurial solution. As we said before, the print has not been bleached in reality—the substance which originally formed it is still there, together with a new substance, a salt of mercury. But the two salts of silver and mercury may be easily brought out and made visible by several solutions, such as sulphide of ammonium, solution of hydrosulphuric acid ; in fact, any of the soluble sulphides, ammonia and hyposulphite of soda. The latter salt is used in preference to the others. Small pieces of blotting-paper, therefore, of the same size as the prints, are cut out and steeped in a saturated solution of hyposulphite of soda and then dried. The magic photographs are packed as before stated, between folds of orange-colored paper ; the papers dipped in hyposulphite of soda are the developers, and may be packed between two sheets of common writing-paper. The development of the image is effected in the following manner : place the albumen paper which contains the whitened print on a pane of glass, print side upward ; on this lay the dry piece of blotting-paper that has been previously dipped in hyposulphite of soda. Moisten the latter thoroughly, then place over it a pane of glass, and upon this a weight, to bring the two pieces of paper into intimate contact. In a very short time the picture will appear in all its original detail, and of a sepia tone.

Writing on the Arm.—The conjurer's explanation was a great lesson in " spiritualism." I next asked him to elucidate the trick of writing on the arm. On the occasion of my visit to Mr. Forster, when the raps indicated the second pellet, he required the "spirit" present to write the initials on his bare arm. Mr. Forster placed his arm under the table for a moment, then rested it in front of a lamp burning on the table, and quickly rolled up the sleeve of his coat. The skin was without stain or mark. He passed his hand over it once or twice, and the initials of the names I had written on the second pellet seemed to grow on the arm in letters of crimson. "It's a trick I do every night. It goes with the audience like steam," said the conjurer. " Very simple. Well, suppose a name. What name would you like ?" " Henry Clay," I replied. Down went the conjurer's arm under the table. In a few seconds he raised it and exposed the bare forearm without mark upon it. He doubled up his fist tightly so as to bring the muscles of the arm to the surface, and rubbed the skin smartly with his open hand. The letters " H. C." soon appeared upon it in well-defined writing of a deep red color. "There you have it, gentlemen ; that's the blood-red writing. Very simple. All you have to do is take a lucifer match, and write on your arm with the wrong end of it. If you moisten the skin with a little salt water first, all the better. Then wet the palm of the other hand, rub your arm with it. Send up the muscles and the blood-red writing will come out. It will fade away in less than no time. If you look under the table, you will see that I have a little piece of pointed wood. I can move my arm under that and write the letters without using the other hand. But that's a trick which wants practice.

Electrical Psychology.—The most easy and direct mode to produce electro psychological communication is to take the individual by the hand, in the same manner as though you were going to shake hands. Press your thumb on the *Ulnar nerve,* which spreads its branches to the ring and little finger, an inch above the knuckle, and in range of the ring finger. Lay the ball of the thumb flat so as to cover the minute branches of this nerve of motion and sensation. When you first take him by the hand, request him to place his eyes upon yours, and to keep them fixed, so that he may see every emotion of your mind expressed in the countenance. Continue this pressure for a half a minute or more. Then request him to close his eyes, and with your fingers gently brush downward several times over the eyelids. Throughout the whole process feel within yourself a fixed determination to close them, so as to express that determination fully in your countenance and manner. Then place your hand on the top of his head and press your thumb firmly on the organ of Individuality, bearing partially downward, and with the other thumb still pressing the ulnar nerve, tell him —*you can not open your eyes!* Remember, that your manner, your expression of countenance, your motions, and your language must all be of the most positive character. If he succeed in opening his eyes, try it once or twice more, because impressions, whether physical or mental, continue to deepen by repetition. In case, however, that you cannot close his eyes, nor see any effect produced upon them, you should cease making any further efforts, because you have now fairly tested that his mind and body both stand in a positive relation as it regards the doctrine of impressions. If you succeed in closing the subject's eyes by the above mode, you may then request him to put his hands on his head, or in any other position you choose, and tell him, *you can not stir them!* In case you succeed, request him to be seated, and tell him, *you can not rise!* If you are successful in this, request him to put his hands in motion, and tell him, *you can not stop them!* If you succeed, request him to walk the floor, and tell him, *you can not cease walking!* And so you may continue to perform experiments involving muscular motion and paralysis of any kind that may occur to your mind, till you can completely control him, in arresting or moving all the voluntary parts of his system.

How to Make Persons at a Distance Think of You.—Let it be particularly remembered that " Faith" and concentration of thought are positively needful to accomplish aught in drawing others to you or making them think of you. If you have not the capacity or understanding how to operate an electric telegraph battery, it is no proof that an expert and competent person should fail doing so; just so in this case; if faith, meditation, or concentration of thought fail you, then will you also fail to operate upon others. First, you must have an yearning for the person you wish to make think of you; and secondly, you must learn to guess at what time of day or night he may be unemployed, passive, so that he be in a proper state to receive the thought which you dispatch to him. If he should be occupied in any way, so that his nervous forces were needed to complete his task, his :" Human Battery," or thought, would not be in a recipient or passive condition, therefore your experiment would fail at that moment. Or if he were under heavy narcotics, liquors, tobacco, or gluttonous influences, he could not be reached at such moments. Or, if he were asleep, and you operated to affect a wakeful mind or thought, you would fail again at the moment. To make a person at a distance think of you, whether you are acquainted with him or not, matters not; I again repeat, find out or guess at what moment he is likely to be pas-sive; by this I mean easy and careless: then, with the most fervent prayer, or yearning of your entire heart, mind, soul and strength, desire he may think of you; and if you wish him to think on any particular topic in relation to you, it is necessary for you to press your hands, when operating on him, on such mental faculties of your head as you wish him to exercise towards you. This demands a meagre knowledge of Phrenology. His "Feeling Nature," or "Propensities," you cannot reach through these operations, but when he once thinks of you, (if he does not know you he imagines such a being as you are,) he can easily afterwards be controlled by you, and he will feel disposed to go in the direction where you are, if circumstances permit, and he is his own master, for, remember, circumstances alter cases. I said, you cannot reach his "Feeling," but only his "Thinking Nature," truly, but after he thinks of you once, his "Feeling Nature," or propensities, may become aroused through his own organization. In conclusion on this topic, let me say, that if you wish the person simply to think of you, one operation may answer; but on the contrary, if you wish him to meet you, or go where you are, all you have to do is to persevere in a lawful and Christian manner to operate, and I assure you, in the course of all natural things, that is, if no accident or very unfavorable circumstances occur, he will make his way towards you, and when he comes within sight, or reaching distance of you, it will be easy to manage him.

How to Make Large Noses Small.—Dr. Cid, an inventive surgeon of Paris, noticed that elderly people, who for a long time have

worn eyeglasses supported on the nose by a spring, are apt to have
this organ long and thin. This he attributes to the compression
which the spring exerts on the arteries by which the nose is nour-
ished. The idea occurred to him that the hint could be made useful. Not long afterward, a young lady of fifteen years consulted
him, to see if he could restore to moderate dimensions her nose,
which was large, fleshy, and unsightly. The trait, he found, was
hereditary in her family, as her mother and sister were similarly
afflicted. This was discouraging, as hereditary peculiarities are
particularly obstinate. But the doctor determined to try his
method; he took exact measurements, and had constructed for
her a " lunette pince-nez "—a spring and pad for compressing the
artery—which she wore at night and whenever she could conveniently in daytime. In three weeks a consolatory diminution was
evident, and in three months the young lady was quite satisfied
with the improvement in her features.

Jockey Tricks.—*How to make a horse appear as though he was badly
Foundered.*—Take a fine wire and fasten it tight around the fet-
lock, between the foot and the heel, and smooth the hair over it.
In twenty minutes the horse will show lameness.—Do not leave it
on over nine hours.—*To make a horse lame.*—Take a single hair
from his tail, put it through the eye of a needle, then lift the front
leg, and press the skin between the outer and the middle tendon or
cord, and shove the needle through, cut off the hair each side and
let the foot down; the horse will go lame in twenty minutes.—*How
to make a horse stand by his food and not take it.*—Grease the front
teeth and the roof of the mouth with common beef tallow, and he
will not eat until you wash it out; this in conjunction with the
above will consummate a complete founder.—*How to cure a horse
from the crib or sucking wind.*—Saw between the upper teeth to
the gums.—*How to put a young countenance on a horse.*—Make a small
incision in the sunken place over the eye, insert the point of a
goose quill and blow it up; close the external wound with thread
and it is done.—*To cover up the heaves.*—Drench the horse with one-
fourth pound of common bird shot, and he will not heave until
they pass through him.—*To make a horse appear as if he had the
glanders.*—Melt four ounces of fresh butter and pour it into his ear.
—*To distinguish between distemper and glanders.*—The discharge from
the nose in glanders will sink in water; in distemper it floats.—
How to make a true pulling horse baulk.—Take tincture of cantharides one ounce, and corrosive sublimate one drachm; mix, and
bathe his shoulder at night.—*How to nerve a horse that is lame.*—
Make a small incision about half way from the knee to the joint
on the outside of the leg, and at the back part of the shin bone
you will find a small white tendon or cord, cut it off and close the
external wound with a stitch, and he will walk off on the hardest
pavement and not limp a particle.

To Bore Holes in Glass.—Any hard steel tool will cut glass with great facility when kept freely wet with camphor dissolved in turpentine. A drill-bow may be used, or even the hand alone. A hole bored may be readily enlarged by a round file. The ragged edges of glass vessels may also be thus easily smoothed by a flat file. Flat window glass can readily be sawed by a watch spring saw by aid of this solution. In short, the most brittle glass can be wrought almost as easily as brass by the use of cutting tools kept constantly moist with camphorized oil of turpentine.

To Etch upon Glass.—Procure several thick, clear pieces of crown glass, and immerse them in melted wax, so that each may receive a complete coating, or pour over them a solution of wax in benzine. When perfectly cold draw on them, with a fine steel point, flowers, trees, houses, portraits, etc. Whatever parts of the drawing are intended to be corroded with the acid, should be perfectly free from the least particle of wax. When all these drawings are finished the pieces of glass must be immersed one by one in a square leaden box or receiver, where they are to be submitted to the action of hydrofluoric acid gas, made by acting on powdered fluor-spar by concentrated sulphuric acid.

FARMERS' DEPARTMENT.

How to get New Varieties of Potatoes.—When the vines are done growing and are turned brown; the seed is ripe: then take the balls and string with a large needle and strong thread; hang them in a dry place where they will gradually dry and mature, without danger or injury from frost. In the month of April, soak the ball for several hours from the pulp; when washed and dried, they are fit for sowing in rows, in a bed well prepared in the garden; they will sprout in a fortnight; they must be attended to like other vegetables. When about two inches high, they may be thinned and transplanted into rows. As they increase in size, they should be hilled. In the autumn many of them will be of the size of a walnut, and from that to a pea. In the following spring they should be planted in hills, placing the large ones together,—they will in the second season attain their full size, and will exhibit several varieties of form, and may then be selected to suit the judgment of the cultivator. I would prefer gathering the balls from potatoes of a good kind. The first crops from seeds thus obtained will be productive, and will continue so for many years, gradually deteriorating, until they will need a renewal by the process.

To Destroy Rats.—Fill any deep smooth vessel of considerable capacity to within six inches of the top with water, cover the surface with bran, and set the vessel in a place most frequented by these pests. In attempting to get at the bran they will fall in and be drowned. Several dozen have been taken by this simple method at a time.

To Kill Rats in Barn and Rick.—Melt hog's lard in a bottle plunged in water of temperature of 150 degrees Fahrenheit: introduce into it half an ounce of phosphorus for every pound of lard; then add a pint of proof spirits or whiskey; cork the bottle firmly after its contents have been to 150 degrees, taking it out of the water and agitating till the phosphorus becomes uniformly diffused, making a milky looking fluid. The spirit may be poured off on the liquor cooling; and you then have a fatty compound, which, after being warmed gently, may be incorporated with a mixture of wheat flour, or sugar, flavored with oil of rhodium, or oil of anise-seed, etc., and the dough, on being made into pellets, should be laid at the rat holes; being luminous in the dark, and agreeable both to the palates and noses, it is readily eaten, and proves certainly fatal. The rats issue from their holes and seek for water to quench their burning thirst, and they commonly die near the water.

Rat Poison.—Flour, six pounds; sugar, one pound; sulphur, four pounds; phosphorus, four pounds.

To Banish and Prevent Mosquitoes from Biting.—Dilute a little of the oil of thyme with sweet oil, and dip pieces of paper in it. Hang in your room, or rub a little on the hands and face when going to bed.

To Keep Milk Sweet in the Hottest Weather.—Put a spoonful of horse-radish in a pan of milk; this will keep it sweet for several days longer than without.

RECIPES FOR HORSES.

Blistering Liniment.—Powdered Spanish flies, one ounce; spirits turpentine, six ounces. Rub on the belly for pain in the bowels, or on the surface for internal inflammation.

Cathartic Powder.—To cleanse out horses in the spring, making them sleek and healthy; black sulphuret of antimony, nitre, and sulphur, each equal parts. Mix well together, and give a tablespoonful every morning.

Cough Ball for Horses.—Pulverized ipecac, three-quarters of an ounce; camphor, two ounces; squills, half an ounce. Mix with honey to form into mass, and divide into eight balls. Give one every morning.

Diuretic Balls.—Castile soap scraped fine, powdered resin, each three teaspoonfuls; powdered nitre, four teaspoonfuls; oil of juniper, one small teaspoonful: honey, a sufficient quantity to make into a ball.

To prevent Horses being Teased by Flies.—Boil three handfuls of walnut leaves in three quarts of water; sponge the horse (before going out of the stable) between and upon the ears, neck and flank.

To Prevent Botts.—Mix a little wood-ashes with their drink daily. This effectually preserves horses against the botts.

Liniment for Galled Backs of Horses.—White lead moistened with milk. When milk cannot be procured, oil may be substituted. One or two ounces will last two months or more.

Remedy for Strains in Horses.—Take whiskey, one half pint: camphor, one ounce; sharp vinegar, one pint. Mix. Bathe the parts affected.

Another.—Take opodeldoc, warm it, and rub the strained part two or three times a day.

Lotion for Blows, Bruises, Sprains, etc.—One part laudanum, two parts oil origanum, four parts water ammonia, four parts oil of turpentine, four parts camphor, thirty-two parts spirits of wine. Put them into a bottle, and shake them until mixed.

Fever Ball.—Emetic tartar and camphor, each half an ounce; nitre, two ounces. Mix with linseed meal and molasses to make eight balls. Give one twice a day.

Liniment for Sprains, Swellings, etc.—Aqua ammonia, spirits camphor, each, two ounces; oil origanum and laudanum, each, half an ounce. Mix.

Lotion for Mange.—Boil two ounces tobacco in one quart water: strain; add sulphur and soft soap, each, two ounces.

Purgative Ball.—Aloes, one ounce; cream tartar and castile soap, one uarter of an ounce. Mix with molasses to make a ball.

CONFECTIONERS' DEPARTMENT.

Ginger Candy.—Boil a pound of clarified sugar until, upon taking a drop of it on a piece of stick, it will become brittle when cold. Mix and stir up with it, for a common article, about a teaspoonful of ground ginger; if for a superior article, instead of the ground ginger add half the white of an egg, beaten up previously with fine sifted loaf sugar, and twenty drops of strong essence of ginger.

Ginger Lozenges.—Dissolve in one-quarter of a pint of hot water half an ounce of gum arabic; when cold, stir it up with one and a half pounds of loaf sugar. and a spoonful of powdered ginger, or twelve drops of essence of ginger. Roll and beat the whole up into a paste; make it into a flat cake, and punch out the lozenges with a round stamp; dry them near the fire, or in an oven.

Peppermint Lozenges.—Best powdered white sugar, seven pounds; pure starch, one pound; oil of peppermint to flavor. Mix with mucilage.

Peppermint, Rose or Hoarhound Candy.—They may be made as lemon candy. Flavor with essence of rose or peppermint or finely powdered hoarhound. Pour it out in a buttered paper, placed in a square tin pan.

To Clarify Sugar for Candies.—To every pound of sugar, put a large cup of water, and put it in a brass or copper kettle, over a slow fire, for half an hour; pour into it a small quantity of isinglass and gum Arabic, dissolved together. This will cause all impurities to rise to the surface; skim it as it rises. Flavor according to taste.

All kinds of sugar for candy, are boiled as above directed. When boiling loaf sugar, add a tablespoonful of rum or vinegar, to prevent its becoming too brittle whilst making.

Loaf sugar when boiled, by pulling and making into small rolls, and twisting a little, will make what is called little rock, or snow. By pulling loaf sugar after it is boiled, you can make it as white as snow.

Common Twist Candy.—Boil three pounds of common sugar and one pint of water over a slow fire for half an hour, without skimming. When boiled enough take it off; rub the hands over with butter; take that which is a little cooled, and pull it as you would molasses candy, until it is white; then twist or braid it, and cut it up in strips.

Fine Peppermint Lozenges.—Best powdered white sugar, 7 pounds; pure starch, 1 pound; oil of peppermint to flavor. Mix with mucilage.

Everton Taffee.—To make this favorite and wholesome candy, take 1½ pounds of moist sugar, 3 ounces of butter, a teacup and a half of water and one lemon. Boil the sugar, butter, water, and half the rind of the lemon together, and when done—which will be known by dropping into cold water, when it should be quite crisp—let it stand aside till the boiling has ceased, and then stir in the juice of the lemon. Butter a dish, and pour it in about a quarter of an inch in thickness. The fire must be quick, and the taffee stirred all the time.

Candy Fruit.—Take 1 pound of the best loaf sugar; dip each lump into a bowl of water, and put the sugar into your preserving kettle. Boil it down and skim it until perfectly clear, and in a candying state. When sufficiently boiled, have ready the fruits you wish to preserve. Large white grapes, oranges separated into small pieces, or preserved fruits, taken out of their syrup and dried, are very nice. Dip the fruits into the prepared sugar while it is hot; put them in a cold place; they will soon become hard.

Popped Corn.—Dipped in boiling molasses and stuck together forms an excellent candy.

Molasses Candy.—Boil molasses over a moderately hot fire, stirring constantly. When you think it is done, drop a little on a plate, and if sufficiently boiled it will be hard. Add a small quantity of vinegar to render it brittle and any flavoring ingredient you prefer. Pour in buttered tin pans. If nuts are to be added strew them in the pans before pouring out the candy.

Liquorice Lozenges..—Extract of liquorice, 1 pound, powdered white sugar, 2 pounds. Mix with mucilage made with rosewater,

Fig Candy.—Take 1 pound of sugar and 1 pint of water, set over a slow fire. When done, add a few drops of vinegar and a lump of butter, and pour into pans in which split figs are laid.

Raisin Candy.—Can be made in the same manner, substituting stoned raisins for the figs. Common molasses candy is very nice with all kinds of nuts added.

Scotch Butter Candy.—Take 1 pound of sugar, 1 pint of water: dissolve and boil. When done add 1 tablespoonful of butter, and enough lemon juice and oil of lemon to flavor.

Icing for Cakes.—Beat the whites of two small eggs to a high froth; then add to them a quarter of a pound of white, ground, or powdered sugar; beat it well until it will lie in a heap; flavor with lemon or rose. This will frost the top of a common-sized cake. Heap what you suppose to be sufficient in the centre of the cake, then dip a broad-bladed knife in cold water, and spread the ice evenly over the whole surface.

Saffron Lozenges.—Finely powdered hay-saffron, 1 ounce; finely powdered sugar, 1 pound; finely powdered starch, 8 ounces. Mucilage to mix.

Chocolate Cream.—Chocolate, scraped fine, ½ ounce; thick cream, 1 pint; sugar (best), 3 ounces; heat it nearly to boiling, then remove it from the fire, and mill it well. When cold add the whites of four or five eggs; whisk rapidly and take up the froth on a sieve; serve the cream in glasses, and pile up the froth on the top of them.

Candied Lemon or Peppermint for Colds.—Boil 1½ pounds sugar in a half pint of water, till it begins to candy around the sides; put in 8 drops of essence; pour it upon buttered paper, and cut it with a knife.

VALUABLE MISCELLANEOUS RECEIPTS, FOR THE HOUSEHOLD AND EVERY DAY REQUIREMENTS.

Alum in Starch.—For starching muslins, ginghams, and calicoes, dissolve a piece of alum the size of a shellbark, for every pint of starch, and add to it. By so doing the colors will keep bright for a long time, which is very desirable when dresses must be often washed, and the cost is but a trifle.

Cider Yeast.—Take cider from sour apples before it ferments, scald, skim thoroughly, and pour, while hot, upon flour enough to make a stiff batter. When cool, add yeast of any kind, and let it rise, stirring it down as often as it tries to run over for several days, then put it in a cool place (where it will not freeze), and you will have something equal to the best hop yeast. It will keep until May without any further labor.

To Destroy Cockroaches.—The following is said to be effectual: These vermin are easily destroyed, simply by cutting up green cucumbers at night, and placing them about where roaches commit depredations. What is cut from the cucumbers in preparing them for the table answers the purpose as well, and three applications will destroy all the roaches in the house. Remove the peelings in the morning, and renew them at night.

Fire Kindlers.—Take a quart of tar and three pounds of resin, melt them, bring to a cooling temperature, mix with as much sawdust, with a little charcoal added, as can be worked in; spread out while hot upon a board, when cold break up into lumps of the size of a large hickory nut, and you have, at a small expense, kindling

material enough for a household for one year. They will easily
ignite from a match and burn with a strong blaze, long enough to
start any wood that is fit to burn.

Remedy against Moths.—An ounce of gum camphor and one of the
powdered shell of red pepper are macerated in eight ounces of
strong alcohol for several days, then strained. With this tincture
the furs or cloths are sprinkled over, and rolled up in sheets. Instead of the pepper, bitter apple may be used. This remedy is
used in Russia under the name of the Chinese tincture for moths.

Substitute for Yeast.—Boil one pound of flour, one quarter pound
of brown sugar and a little salt in two gallons of water for one
hour. When milk-warm, bottle and cork close, and it will be
ready for use in twenty-four hours.

To make Ley.—Have a large tub or cask and bore a hole on one
side for a tap, near the bottom ; place several bricks near the hole
and cover them with straw. Fill the barrel with strong wood
ashes. Oak ashes are strongest, and those of appletree wood
make the whitest soap. Pour on boiling water until it begins to
run, then put in the tap and let it soak. If the ashes settle down
as they are wet, fill in until full.

Tomato Wine.—Take ripe, fresh tomatoes, mash very fine, strain
through a fine sieve, sweeten with good sugar, to suit the taste,
set it away in an earthen or glass vessel, nearly full, cover tight,
with exception of a small hole for the refuse to work off through
during its fermentation. When it is done fermenting it will become pure and clear. Then bottle, and cork tight. A little salt
improves it flavor ; age improves it.

To Color Brown on Cotton or Woolen.—For ten pounds of cloth
boil three pounds of catechu in as much water as needed to cover
the goods. When dissolved, add four ounces of blue vitriol ; stir
it well ; put in the cloth and let it remain all night ; in the morning drain it thoroughly ; put four ounces of bi-chromate of potash
in boiling water sufficient to cover your goods ; let it remain 15
minutes ; wash in cold water ; color in iron.

To Cleanse and Brighten Faded Brussels Carpet.—Boil some bran in
water and with this wash the carpet with a flannel and brush, using fuller's earth for the worst parts. When dry, the carpet must
be well beaten to get out the fuller's earth, then washed over with
a weak solution of alum to brighten the colors. Some housekeep-
ers cleanse and brighten carpets by sprinkling them first with fine
salt and then sweeping them thoroughly.

To give Stoves a Fine, Brilliant Appearance.—A teaspoonful of pulverized alum mixed with stove polish will give a stove a fine luster, which will be quite permanent.

Method of Keeping Hams in Summer.—Make bags of unbleached muslin; place in the bottom a little good sweet hay; put in the ham, and then press around and over it firmly more hay; tie the bag and hang up in a dry place. Ham secured in this way will keep for years.

How to Cause Vegetables and Fruits to Grow to an Enormous Size and also to Increase the Brilliancy and Fragrancy of Flowers.—A curious discovery has recently been made public in France, in regard to the culture of vegetable and fruit trees. By watering with a solution of sulphate of iron, the most wonderful fecundity has been attained. Pear-trees and beans, which have been submitted to this treatment, have nearly doubled in the size of their productions, and a noticeable improvement has been remarked in their flavor. Dr. Becourt reports that while at the head of an establishment at Enghien, or the sulphurous springs, he had the gardens and plantations connected with it watered, during several weeks of the early Spring, with sulphurous water, and that not only the plantations prospered to a remarkable extent, but flowers acquired a peculiar brilliancy of coloring and healthy aspect which attracted universal attention.

Drying Corn.—With a sharp knife shave the corn from the ear, then scrape the cob, leaving one-half the hull clinging to the cob. Place a tin or earthen vessel two-thirds full of this "milk of corn" over a kettle of boiling water, stir frequently until dry enough to spread upon a firm cloth without sticking, when the wind and sun (away from dust and flies) will soon complete the process. To prepare for the table, put in cold water, set it where it will become hot, but not boil, for two hours; then season with salt and pepper, boil for ten minutes; add of butter and white sugar a tablespoonful of each just before ready to serve.

To Destroy Lice on Chickens.—The following will kill lice on the first application: Put six cents worth of cracked *Coculus Indicus* berries into a bottle that will hold a half pint of alcohol: fill the bottle with alcohol, and let it stand twenty-four hours. When the hen comes off with the young chickens, take the mixture, and with a small cotton rag, wet the head of each chicken enough to have it reach through the little feathers to the skin; also, with the same rag, wet the hen under her wings. Be careful that no child, nor any one else uses it, because it a *deadly poison.*

Cracked Wheat.—For a pint of the cracked grain, have two quarts of water boiling in a smooth iron pot over a quick fire; stir in the wheat slowly; boil fast and stir constantly for the first half hour of cooking, or until it begins to thicken and "pop up;" then lift from the quick fire, and place the pot where the wheat will cook slowly for an hour longer. Keep it covered closely, stir now and then, and be careful not to let it burn at the bottom. Wheat cooked thus is much sweeter and richer than when left to soak and simmer for hours, as many think necessary. White wheat cooks the easiest. When ready to dish out, have your moulds moistened with cold water, cover lightly, and set in a cool place. Eat warm or cold with milk and sugar.

How to Have Green Pea Soup in Winter.—Sow peas thickly in pots and boxes, say six weeks before the soup is wanted. Place them in a temperature of 60° or so, close to the glass in a house or pit. Cut the plants as soon as they attain a height of from three to six inches, and rub them through a sieve. The shoots alone will make a fair soup. Mixed with dry peas, also passed through a sieve, no one could scarcely distinguish color or flavor from that of real green pea soup. There is, however, considerable difference in the flavor of pea leaves, as well as of the peas themselves. The best marrows, such as Ne Plus Ultra and Veitche's Perfection, yield the most piquant cuttings. Also the more light the plants receive the higher the flavor, plants drawn up or at all blanched, being by no means comparable with those well and strongly grown.

In the spring, a few patches or rows may be sown in open quarters expressly for green cuttings. These are most perfect and full flavored when four inches high. When too long, the flavor seems to have run to wood, and the peculiar aroma of green peas is weaker.

There is yet another mode of making green pea soup at any season at very short notice. Chip the peas by steeping them in water and leaving them in a warm place for a few days. Then slightly boil or stew, chips and all, and pass them through a sieve. The flavor is full and good, though such pea soup lacks color. It is astonishing how much the mere vegetation of seeds develops their more active and predominant flavor or qualities; a fact that might often be turned to useful account in the kitchen in the flavoring of soups or dishes, with turnips, celery, parsley, etc.

Composition for Restoring Scorched Linen.—Boil, to a good consistency, in half a pint of vinegar, two ounces of fuller's earth, an ounce of hen's dung, half an ounce of cake soap, and the juice of two onions. Spread this composition over the whole of the damaged part; and if the scorching is not quite through, and the threads actually consumed, after suffering it to dry on, and letting it receive a subsequent good washing or two, the place will appear full as white and perfect as any other part of the linen.

To Remove Indelible Ink Stains.—Soak the stained spot in strong salt water, then wash it with ammonia. Salt changes the nitrate of silver into chloride of silver, and ammonia dissolves the chloride.

To Cook Cauliflower.—Choose those that are close and white and of middle size, trim off the outside leaves, cut the stalk off flat at the bottom, let them lie in salt and water an hour before you boil them. Put them into boiling water with a handful of salt in it, skim it well and let it boil slowly till done. Fifteen minutes will suffice for a small one, and twenty will be long enough for a large one. If it is boiled a minute or two after it is done the flavor will be impaired.

To Pickle String Beans.—Place them in a pan with alternate layers of salt and leave them thus for 24 hours. Drain them and place them in a jar with allspice, cloves, pepper and a little salt. Boil enough vinegar to cover them, pour over them and let them stand till the next day, boil the vinegar the second time, and pour it on again. The next day boil the vinegar for the last time, pour it over the beans, and when quite cold, cover the jar tightly and set in a cool closet.

How to Cause a Baby to Thrive and Grow.—Try the milk first drawn from a cow that is fresh, add one-quarter water, and a little sugar. If the milk constipates, sweeten it with molasses, or mix with it a small quantity of magnesia. Abjure soothing syrups, and for colic give catnip or smellage tea. Give the baby a tepid bath at night as well as in the morning, rubbing him well with the hand. After the bath, let him feed and then sleep. We find open air the best of tonics for babies. Our's takes his naps out of doors in the shade during the warm weather, and his cheeks are two roses.

To Can Gooseberries without Breaking them.—Fill the cans with berries, and partly cover with water, set the jars into a vessel of water, and raise the temperature to the boiling point. Boil eight minutes, remove from the kettle, cover with boiling water, and seal immediately. If sugar is used, let it be pure white, and allow eight ounces to a quart of berries. Make into a syrup, and use in the cans instead of water. The glass cans with glass tops, a rubber and a screw ring, we have found the simplest and most perfect of the many kinds offered for sale in the market.

Ready Mode of Mending Cracks in Stoves, Pipes and Iron Ovens.—When a crack is discovered in a stove, through which the fire or smoke penetrates, the aperture may be completely closed in a moment with a composition consisting of wood ashes and common salt made up into paste with a little water, and plastered over the crack. The good effect is equally certain, whether the stove, etc., be cold or hot.

To Keep Milk from Turning Sour.—Add a little sub-carbonate of soda, or of potash. This by combining with, and neutralizing the acetic acid formed, has the desired effect, and keeps the milk from turning sooner than it otherwise would. The addition is perfectly harmless, and does not injure the taste.

Strawberry Vinegar.—Put four pounds of very ripe strawberries, nicely dressed, into three quarts of the best vinegar, and let them stand three or four days; then drain the vinegar through a jelly-bag, and pour it on the same quantity of fruit. Repeat the process in three days for a third time. Finally, to each pound of the liquor thus obtained, add one pound of fine sugar. Bottle, and let it stand covered, but not tightly corked, one week; then cork it tight, and set it in a cool, *dry* place, where it will not freeze. Raspberry vinegar is made the same way.

Cider Vinegar.—After cider has become too sour for use, set it in a warm place, put to it occasionally the rinsings of the sugar basin or molasses jug, and any remains of ale or cold tea; let it remain with the bung open, and you will soon have the best of vinegar.

To Give Luster to Silver.—Dissolve a quantity of alum in water, so as to make a pretty strong brine, and skim it carefully; then add some soap to it, and dip a linen rag in it, and rub over the silver.

To Make Water-Proof Porous Cloth.—Close water-proof cloth fabrics, such as glazed oil-cloth, India-rubber, and gutta-percha cloth are completely water-proof, but do not permit perspiration and the exhaled gases from the skin to pass through them, because they are air-tight as well as water-tight. Persons who wear air-tight garments soon become faint, if they are undergoing severe exercise, such as that to which soldiers are exposed when on march. A porous, water-proof cloth, therefore, is the best for outer garments during wet weather, for those whose duties or labor causes them to perspire freely. The best way for preparing such cloth is by the following process: Take 2¼ pounds of alum and dissolve this in 10 gallons of boiling water; then in a separate vessel dissolve the same quantity of sugar of lead in 10 gallons of water, and mix the two solutions. The cloth is now well handled in this liquid, until every part of it is penetrated; then it is squeezed and dried in the air, or in a warm apartment, then washed in cold water and dried again, when it is fit for use. If necessary, the cloth may be dipped in the liquid and dried twice before being washed. The liquor appears curdled, when the alum and lead solutions are mixed together. This is the result of double decomposition, the sulphate of lead, which is an insoluble salt, being formed. The sulphate of lead is taken up in the pores of the cloth, and it is unaffected by rains or moisture, and yet it does not render the cloth air-tight. Such cloth is also partially non-inflammable. A solution of alum itself will render cloth, prepared as described, partially water-proof, but it is not so good as the sulphate of lead. Such cloth—cotton or woolen—sheds rain like the feathers on the back of a duck.

To Cleanse Carpet.—1 teaspoonful liquid ammonia in one gallon warm water, will often restore the color of carpets, even if produced by acid or alkali. If a ceiling has been whitewashed with the carpet down, and a few drops are visible, this will remove it. Or, after the carpet is well beaten and brushed, scour with ox gall, which will not only extract grease but freshen the colors—1 pint of gall in 3 gallons of warm water, will do a large carpet. Table floor-cloths may be thus washed. The suds left from a wash where ammonia is used, even if almost cold, cleanses these floor-cloths well.

To Keep Hams.—After the meat has been well cured by pickle and smoke, take some clean ashes from bits of coal; moisten them with a little water so that they will form a paste, or else just wet the hams a ltttle, and rub on the dry ashes. Rubbed in thoroughly they serve as a capital insect protector, and the hams can be hung up in the smoke-house or wood-chamber without any danger of molestation.

A Cold Cement for Mending Earthenware, says a recent English work, reckoned a great secret among workmen, is made by grating a pound of old cheese, with a bread grater, into a quart of milk, in which it must be left for a period of fourteen hours. It should be stirred quite often. A pound of unslaked lime, finely pulverized in a mortar, is then added, and the whole is thoroughly mixed by beating. This done, the whites of 25 eggs are incorporated with the rest, and the whole is ready for use. There is another cement for the same purpose which is used hot. It is made of resin, beeswax, brick-dust, and chalk boiled together. The substances to be cemented must be heated, and when the surfaces are coated with cement, they must be rubbed hard upon each other, as in making a glue-joint with wood.

How to Make Cucumber Vines Bear Five Crops.—When a cucumber is taken from the vine let it be cut with a knife, leaving about the eighth of an inch of the cucumber on the stem, then slit the stem with a knife from the end to the vine, leaving a small portion of the cucumber on each division, and on each separate slit there will be a new cucumber as large as the first.

White Cement.—Take white (fish) glue, 1 lb. 10 oz.; dry white lead, 6 oz.; soft water, 3 pts.; alcohol, 1 pt.

Dissolve the glue by putting it in a tin kettle or dish, containing the water, and set this dish in a kettle of water, to prevent the glue from being burned; when the glue is all dissolved, put in the lead and stir and boil until it is thoroughly mixed; remove from the fire, and when cool enough to bottle, add the alcohol, and bottle while it is yet warm, keeping it corked. This last recipe has been sold about the country for from twenty-five cents to five dollars, and one man gave a horse for it.

Bruises on Furniture.—Wet the part in warm water; double a piece of brown paper five or six times, soak in the warm water, and lay it on the place; apply on that a warm, but not hot, flatiron till the moisture is evaporated. If the bruise be not gone repeat the process. After two or three applications the dent will be raised to the surface. If the bruise be small, merely soak it with warm water, and hold a red-hot iron near the surface, keeping the surface continually wet—the bruise will soon disappear.

To Prevent Iron Rust.—Kerosene applied to stoves or farming implements, during summer, will prevent their rusting.

To Color Sheep Skins.—Unslaked lime and litharge equal parts, mixed to a thin paste with water, will color buff—several coats will make it a dark brown; by adding a little ammonia and nitrate of silver a fine black is produced. Terra japonica will impart a "tan color" to wool, and the red shade is deepened by sponging with a solution of lime and water, using a strong solution of alum water to "set" the colors; 1 part crystallized nitrate silver, 8 parts carbonate ammonia, and $1\frac{1}{2}$ parts of soft water dyes brown; every additional coat darkens the color until a black is obtained.

Remedy for Burns.—Take one teacup of lard and the whites of two eggs; work together as much as it can be, then spread on cloths and apply. Change as often as necessary.

How Summer Suits should be Washed.—Summer suits are nearly all made of white or buff linen, pique, cambric, or muslin, and the art of preserving the new appearance after washing is a matter of the greatest importance. Common washerwomen spoil everything with soda, and nothing is more frequent than to see the delicate tints of lawns and percales turned into dark blotches and muddy streaks by the ignorance and vandalism of a laundress. It is worth while for ladies to pay attention to this, and insist upon having their summer dresses washed according to the directions which they should be prepared to give their laundresses themselves. In the first place, the water should be tepid, the soap should not be allowed to touch the fabric; it should be washed and rinsed quick, turned upon the wrong side, and hung in the shade to dry, and when starched (in thin boiled but not boiling starch) should be folded in sheets or towels, and ironed upon the wrong side as soon as possible. But linen should be washed in water in which hay or a quart bag of bran has been boiled. This last will be found to answer for starch as well, and is excellent for print dresses of all kinds, but a handful of salt is very useful also to set the colors of light cambrics and dotted lawns; and a little ox gall will not only set but brighten yellow and purple tints, and has a good effect upon green.

How to Fasten Rubber to Wood and Metal.—As rubber plates and rings are now-a-days used almost exclusively for making connections between steam and other pipes and apparatus, much annoyance is often experienced by the impossibility or imperfection of an air-tight connection. This is obviated entirely by employing a cement which fastens alike well to the rubber and to the metal or wood. Such cement is prepared by a solution of shellac in ammonia. This is best made by soaking pulverized gum shellac in ten times its weight of strong ammonia, when a slimy mass is obtained, which in three to four weeks will become liquid without the use of hot water. This softens the rubber, and becomes, after volatilization of the ammonia, hard and impermeable to gases and fluids.

Renewing Maroon Colors on Wool.—Wash the goods in very weak lye; then rinse thoroughly in clear water; thus you have a beautiful, *even* color, although your goods may have been much faded and stained. Though the color thus obtained may not be the exact shade as when new, it is, however, a very pretty one. The above will not answer for other than all woolen goods of a maroon color.

To make Waterproof Cloth out of thick Ducking.—The following French recipe is given : Take two pounds four ounces of alum, and dissolve it in ten gallons of water. In like manner dissolve the same quantity of sugar of lead in a similar quantity of water, and mix the two together. They form a precipitate of the sulphate of lead. The clear liquor is now withdrawn, and the cloth immersed one hour in the solution, when it is taken out and dried in the shade, washed in clean water and dried again.

How to Stop a Pinhole in Lead Pipe.—Take a ten-penny nail, place the square end upon the hole, and hit it two or three slight blows with a hammer, and the orifice is closed as tight as though you had employed a plumber to do it at a cost of a dollar or more.

To Build a Chimney that Will Not Smoke.—The *Scientific American* gives the following hints to those who would "build a chimney which will not smoke":—The chief point is to make the throat not less than four inches broad and twelve long; then the chimney should be abruptly enlarged to double the size, and so continued for one foot or more; then it may be gradually tapered off as desired. But the inside of the chimney, throughout its whole length to the top, should be plastered very smooth with good mortar, which will harden with age. The area of a chimney should be at least half a square foot, and no flues less than sixty square inches. The best shape for a chimney is circular, or many-sided, as giving less friction, (brick is the best material, as it is a non-conductor,) and the higher above the roof the better.

To Prevent Turners' Wood Splitting.—Small pieces of valuable wood, such kinds as are used for turning, etc., are very liable to split readily—that is, outward from the centre. To prevent this, soak the pieces, when first cut, in *cold* water for 24 hours, then boil in hot water for two or three hours, and afterward dry slowly and under cover. This will be found useful in making handsome mantel, toilet, and other articles from sumac, cherry, and other woods that never grow very large.

To Remove Dry Paint on Windows.—The most economical way to remove dry paint from the panes is to make a small swab having a handle some eight inches long, dip it in a little diluted oxalic acid, and rub off the paint with a swab.

Everlasting Fence Posts.—I discovered many years ago that wood could be made to last longer than iron in the ground, but thought the process so simple and inexpensive that it was not worth while making any stir about it. I would as soon have poplar, basswood, or quaking ash as any other kind of timber for fence posts. I have taken out basswood posts after having been set seven years, which were as sound when taken out as when they were first put in the ground. Time and weather seemed to have no effect on them. The posts can be prepared for less than two cents a piece. This is the recipe: Take boiled linseed oil and stir in it pulverized charcoal to the consistency of paint. Put a coat of this over the timber, and there is not a man that will live to see it rotten.

How to Test the Richness of Milk.—Procure any long glass vessel —a cologne bottle or long phial. Take a narrow strip of paper, just the length from the neck to the bottom of the phial, and mark it off with one hundred lines at equal distances; or into fifty lines and count each as two, and paste it upon the phial, so as to divide its length into a hundred equal parts. Fill it to the highest mark with milk fresh from the cow, and allow it to stand in a perpendicular position twenty-four hours. The number of spaces occupied by the cream will give you its exact percentage in the milk without any guess work.

To Remove Stains.—The stains of ink on cloth, paper, or wood may be removed by almost all acids : but those acids are to be preferred which are least likely to injure the texture of the stained substance. The muriatic acid, diluted with five or six times its weight of water, may be applied to the spot, and after a minute or two may be washed off, repeating the application as often as may be necessary. But the vegetable acids are attended with less risk, and are equally effectual. A solution of the oxalic, citric (acid of lemons), or tartareous acids in water may be applied to the most delicate fabrics, without any danger of injuring them; and the same solutions will discharge writing but not printing ink. Hence they may be employed in cleaning books which have been defaced by writing on the margin, without impairing the text. Lemon-juice and the juice of sorrels will also remove ink stains, but not so easily as the concrete acid of lemons or citric acid.

To Prevent Snow-water or Rain from Penetrating the Soles of Shoes or Boots in Winter.—This simple and effectual remedy is nothing more than a little beeswax and mutton suet, warmed in a pipkin until in a liquid state. Then rub some of it lightly over the edges of the sole where the stitches are, which will repel the wet, and not in the least prevent the blacking from having the usual effect.

An Easy Method of Preventing Moths in Furs or Woolens.—Sprinkle the furs or woolen stuffs, as well as the drawers or boxes in which they are kept, with spirits of turpentine; the unpleasant scent of which will speedily evaporate on exposure of the stuffs to the air. Some persons place sheets of paper, moistened with spirits of turpentine, over, under, or between pieces of cloth, etc., and find it a very effectual mode.

To make Sea-water fit for Washing Linen at Sea.—Soda put into sea-water renders it turbid ; the lime and magnesia fall to the bottom. To make sea-water fit for washing linen at sea, as much soda must be put in it, as not only to effect a complete precipitation of these earths, but to render the sea-water sufficiently laxivial or alkaline. Soda should always be taken to sea for this purpose.

To Destroy Insects.—When bugs have obtained a lodgment in walls or timber, the surest mode of overcoming the nuisance is to putty up every hole that is moderately large, and oil-paint the whole wall or timber. In bed-furniture, a mixture of soft soap, with snuff or arsenic, is useful to fill up the holes where the bolts or fastenings are fixed, etc. French polish may be applied to smoother parts of the wood.

Poultice for Burns and Frozen Flesh.—Indian-meal poultices, covered with young hyson tea, moistened with hot water, and laid over burns or frozen parts, as hot as can be borne, will relieve the pain in five minutes ; and blisters, if they have not, will not arise. One poultice is usually sufficient.

Cracked Nipples.—Glycerine and tannin, equal weights, rubbed together into an ointment, is very highly recommended, as is also mutton tallow and glycerine.

To take the Impression of any Butterfly in all its Colors.—Having taken a butterfly, kill it without spoiling its wings, which contrive to spread out as regularly as possible in a flying position. Then, with a small brush or pencil, take a piece of white paper; wash part of it with gum-water, a little thicker than ordinary, so that it may easily dry. Afterwards, laying your butterfly on the paper, cut off the body close to the wings, and, throwing it away, lay the paper on a smooth board with the fly upwards; and, laying another paper over that, put the whole preparation into a screw-press, and screw down very hard, letting it remain under that pressure for half an hour. Afterwards take off the wings of the butterfly, and you will find a perfect impression of them, with all their various colors, marked distinctly, remaining on the paper. When this is done, draw between the wings of your impression the body of the butterfly, and color it after the insect itself.

To take the Stains of Grease from Woolen or Silk.—Three ounces of spirits of wine, three ounces of French chalk powdered, and five ounces of pipe-clay. Mix the above ingredients, and make them up in rolls about the length of a finger, and you will find a never-failing remedy for removing grease from woolen or silken goods. N. B.—It it applied by rubbing on the spot either dry or wet, and afterwards brushing the place.

Easy and Safe Method of Discharging Grease from Woolen Cloths.— Fuller's earth or tobacco pipe-clay, being put wet on an oil-spot, absorbs the oil as the water evaporates, and leaves the vegetable 'or animal fibres of the cloth clean on being beaten or brushed out. When the spot is occasioned by tallow or wax, it is necessary to heat the part cautiously by an iron or the fire while the cloth is drying. In some kinds of goods, blotting-paper, bran, or raw starch, may be used with advantage.

To take out Spots of Ink.—As soon as the accident happens, wet the place with juice of sorrel or lemon, or with vinegar, and the best hard white soap.

To take Iron-moulds out of Linen.—Hold the iron-mould on the cover of a tankard of boiling water, and rub on the spot a little juice of sorrel and a little salt; and when the cloth has thoroughly imbibed the juice, wash it in lye.

To take out Spots on Silk.—Rub the spots with spirits of turpentine; this spirit exhaling, carries off with it the oil that causes the spot.

To take Wax out of Velvet of all Colors except Crimson.—Take a crumby wheaten loaf, cut it in two, toast it before the fire, and, while very hot, apply it to the part spotted with wax. Then apply another piece of toasted bread hot as before, and continue this application until the wax is entirely taken out.

To Bleach Straw.—Straw is bleached by the vapors of sulphur, or a solution of oxalic acid or chloride of lime. It may be dyed with any liquid color.

Windows, to Crystallize.—Dissolve epsom-salts in hot ale, or solution of gum arabic, wash it over the window, and let it dry. If you wish to remove any, to form a border or centre-piece, do it with a wet cloth.

Wax for Bottling.—Rosin, 13 parts; wax, 1 part; melt and add any color. Used to render corks and bungs air-tight by *melting the wax* over them.

Whitewash.—Slack half a bushel of lime with boiling water, and cover the vessel to retain the steam. Strain the liquor, and add one peck of salt previously dissolved in warm water, 3 lbs. of rice boiled and ground to a paste, Spanish whiting, 8 oz.; glue, 1 lb.; mix and add hot water, 5 gallons; let it stand a few days, and apply hot. It makes a brilliant wash for inside or outside works.

To Purify Water for Drinking.—Filter river-water through a sponge, more or less compressed, instead of stone or sand, by which the water is not only rendered more clean, but wholesome; for sand is insensibly dissolved by the water, so that in four or five years it will have lost a fifth part of its weight. Powder of charcoal should be added to the sponge when the water is foul or fetid. Those who examine the large quantity of terrene matter on the inside of tea-kettles, will be convinced all water should be boiled before drunk, if they wish to avoid being afflicted with gravel or stone, etc.

To Purify the Muddy Waters of Rivers or Pits.—Make a number of holes in the bottom of a deep tub; lay some clean gravel thereon, and above this some clean sand; sink this tub in the river or pit, so that only a few inches of the tub will be above the surface of the water; the river or pit water will filter through the sand, and rise clear through it to the level of the water on the outside, and will be pure and limpid.

Method of Making Putrid Water Sweet in a Night's Time.—Four large spoonfuls of unslacked lime, put into a puncheon of ninety gallons of putrid water at sea, will, in one night, make it as clear and sweet as the best spring-water just drawn; but, unless the water is afterwards ventilated sufficiently to carbonize the lime, it will be a lime-water. Three ounces of pure unslacked lime should saturate 90 gallons of water.

To Keep Apples from Freezing.—Apples form an article of chief necessity in almost every family; therefore, great care is taken to protect them from frost; it being well known that they, if left unprotected, are destroyed by the first frost which occurs. They may be kept in the attic with impunity throughout the winter, by simply covering them over with a linen cloth; be sure you have *linen,* for woolen or other cloth is of *no avail.*

To Preserve Grapes.—Take a cask or barrel which will hold water, and put into it, first a layer of bran, dried in an oven, or of ashes well dried and sifted; upon this place a layer of grapes well cleaned, and gathered in the afternoon of a dry day, before they are perfectly ripe; proceed thus with alternate layers of bran or ashes and grapes, till the barrel is full, taking care that the grapes do not touch each other, and to let the last layer be of bran or ashes; then close the barrel so that the air may not penetrate, which is an essential point. Grapes thus packed will keep for nine or even twelve months. To restore them to freshness, cut the end of the stalk of each bunch of grapes, and put it into red wine, as you would flowers into water. White grapes should be put into white wine.

To Increase the Laying of Eggs.—The best method is to mix with their food, every other day, about a teaspoon of ground cayenne pepper to each dozen fowl. Whilst upon this subject, it would be well to say, that if your hens lay soft eggs, or eggs without shells, you should put plenty of old plaster, egg-shells, or even oyster-shells broken up, where they can get at it.

To Preserve Meats.—Beef to pickle for long keeping. First, thoroughly rub salt into it, and let it remain in bulk for twenty-four hours to draw off the blood. Second, take it up, letting it drain, and pack as desired. Third, have ready a pickle prepared as follows: for every 100 pounds of beef use 7 pounds salt; saltpetre and cayenne pepper each, 1 ounce; molasses, 1 quart; and soft water, 8 gallons; boil and skim well, and when cold pour over the beef.

Another method is to use 5 pounds salt, 1 pound brown sugar, and ¼ oz. of saltpetre, to each 100 pounds; dissolve the above in sufficient water to cover the meat, and in two weeks drain all off, and make more same as first. It will then keep through the season. To boil for eating, put into boiling water; for soups, into cold water.

Flies, to Destroy.—Boil some quassia-chips in a little water, sweeten with syrup or molasses, and place it in saucers. It is destructive to flies, but not to children.

Walnuts, to Pickle.—Take 100 young walnuts, lay them in salt and water for two or three days, changing the water every day. (If required to be soon ready for use, pierce each walnut with a larding pin that the pickle may penetrate). Wipe them with a soft cloth, and lay them on a folded cloth for some hours. Then put them in a jar, and pour on them sufficient of the above spiced vinegar, hot, to cover them. Or they may be allowed to simmer gently in strong vinegar, then put into a jar with a handful of mustard-seed, 1 oz. of ginger, ¼ oz. mace, 1 oz. allspice, 2 heads of garlic, and 2 split nutmegs; and pour on them sufficient boiling vinegar to cover them. Some prefer the walnuts to be gently simmered with the brine, then laid on a cloth for a day or two till they turn black, put into a jar, and hot spiced vinegar poured on them.

To Pickle Cucumbers and Gherkins.—Small cucumbers, but not too young, are wiped clean with a dry cloth, put into a jar, and boiling vinegar, with a handful of salt, poured on them. Boil up the vinegar every three days, and pour it on them till they become green: then add ginger and pepper, and tie them up close for use, or cover them with salt and water (as above) in a stone jar; cover them, and set them on the hearth before the fire for two or three days, till they turn yellow; then put away the water, and cover them with hot vinegar, and set them near the fire, and keep them hot for eight or ten days, till they become green; then pour off the vinegar, cover them with hot spiced vinegar, and cover them close.

Mushroom Ketchup.—Pickled mushrooms, 4 lbs.: salt, 2 lbs. Sprinkle it on the mushrooms; and, when they liquefy, remove the juice; add pimento, 6 oz.; cloves, 1 oz.; boil gently and strain: the remaining liquor, if any, may be treated with pepper, mace and ginger for a second quality.

Tomato Ketchup.—Proceed as for mushroom ketchup, and add a little Chili pepper vinegar.

To Take Fac-Similes of Signatures.—Write your name on a piece of paper, and while the ink is wet sprinkle over it some finely-powdered gum arabic, then make a rim round it, and pour on it some fusible alloy, in a liquid state. Impressions may be taken from the plates formed in this way, by means of printing-ink and the copperplate-press.

To Copy Letters without a Press.—A black copying ink, which flows easily from the pen, and will enable any one to obtain very sharp copies without the aid of a press, can be prepared in the following manner: One ounce of coarsely broken extract of logwood and two drachms of crystallized carbonate of soda are placed in a porcelain capsule with eight ounces of distilled water, and heated until the solution is of a deep red color, and all the extract is dissolved. The capsule is then taken from the fire. Stir well into the mixture one ounce of glycerine of specific gravity of 1.25, fifteen grains of neutral chromate of potash, dissolved in a little water, and two drachms of finely pulverized gum arabic, which may be previously dissolved in a little hot water so as to produce a mucilaginous solution. The ink is now complete and ready for use. In well closed bottles it may be kept for a long time without getting mouldy, and, however old it may be, will allow copies of writing to be taken without the aid of a press. It does not attack steel pens. This ink cannot be used with a copying press. Its impression is taken on thin moistened copying paper, at the back of which is placed a sheet of writing paper.

To Obtain Fresh Blown Flowers in Winter.—Choose some of the most perfect buds of the flowers you would preserve, such as are latest in blowing and ready to open; cut them off with a pair of scissors, leaving to each, if possible, a piece of stem about three inches long; cover the end of the stem immediately with sealing wax, and when the buds are a little shrunk and wrinkled, wrap each of them up separately in a piece of paper, perfectly clean and dry, and lock them up in a dry box or drawer; and they will keep without corrupting. In winter, or at any time when you would have the flowers blow, take the buds at night and cut off the end of the stem sealed with wax, and put the buds into water wherein a little nitre or salt has been diffused, and the next day you will have the pleasure of seeing the buds open and expanding themselves, and the flowers display their most lively colors, and breathe their agreeable odors.

Cheap Ice Cream.—Sweet milk, two quarts. Scald the milk, pour over four eggs, and stir well. Cool off and add sugar and essence of lemon or vanilla. Pour into a deep, narrow tin pail. Cover, and set into a wooden pail. Fill up the space between the two vessels with pounded ice and salt. In half an hour it will be fit for use. Keep thus in the ice till wanted to use.

To Take Impressions from Coins.—Make a thick solution of isinglass in water, and lay it hot on the metal; let it remain for twelve hours, then remove it, breathe on it and apply gold or silver-leaf on the wrong side. Any color may be given to the isinglass instead of gold or silver, by simple mixture.

To Print Pictures from the Print Itself.—The page or print is soaked in a solution first of potass, and then of tartaric acid. This produces a perfect diffusion of crystals of bitartrate of potass through the texture of the unprinted part of the paper. As this salt resists oil, the ink roller may now be passed over the surface, without transferring any of its contents, except to the printed paper.

To Preserve Steel Knives from Rust.—Never wrap them in woolen cloths. When they are not to be used for some time, have them made bright and perfectly dry; then take a soft rag, and rub each blade with dry wood ashes.—Wrap them closely in thick brown paper, and lay them in a drawer or dry closet. A set of elegant knives, used only on great occasions, were kept in this way for over a hundred years without a spot of rust.

To Plate and Gild without a Battery.—A very useful solution of silver or gold for plating or gilding without the aid of a battery may be made as follows: Take say, 1 ounce of nitrate of silver, dissolved in one quart of distilled or rain water. When thoroughly dissolved, throw in a few crystals of hyposulphite of soda, which will at first form a brown precipitate, but which eventually becomes redissolved if sufficient hyposulphite has been employed. A slight excess of this salt must, however, be added. The solution thus formed may be used for coating small articles of steel, brass, or German silver, by simply dipping a sponge in the solution and rubbing it over the surface of the article to be coated. I have succeeded in coating steel very satisfactorily by this means, and have found the silver so firmly attached to the steel (when the solution has been carefully made) that it has been removed with considerable difficulty. A solution of gold may be made in the same way, and applied as described. A concentrated solution either of gold or silver thus made, may be used for coating parts of articles which have stripped or blistered, by applying it with a camel hair pencil to the part, and touching the spot at the same time with a thin clean strip of zinc.

To make a Clock for 25 Cents.—First you get a sheet of stout millboard, such as is used by bookbinders. This will cost you from six to ten cents. Get size twenty-seven by twenty-two inches. Draw two lines the longest way equally distant from the edge and each other. This divides it into three parts of the same size. Now from the top measure off ten inches for the face, and then with your knife partly cut the board through the rest of the lines below the face, and bend them back and glue together by putting a strip of cloth over the edges where they meet. Mark out the face of your clock, and make a hole for the hands. Go to your tinman, and he will make you a funnel-shaped spout, which you must glue on the bottom. Then make a spool like a cone—running to a point on one end—and eight inches across on the other. Wind a string on this cone, commencing at the large end, and winding down just as you would a top. Tie to the end a conical ink bottle filled with sand. Make some wooden hands, and put them on the face. Then fill your box, now made, with sand, and when it is hung up the sand will run out slowly at the bottom, and as the sand goes out the weights lower, and turn the wheel, which makes the hands go around. It will depend upon the size of the hole at the bottom as to how fast it runs. You can paint it, and make it quite an ornament and curiosity in your house.

www.ingramcontent.com/pod-product-compliance
Lightning Source LLC
Chambersburg PA
CBHW021524090426
42739CB00007B/763

*9 7 8 3 3 3 7 2 5 6 9 0 6 *